Psychology Hacks

Defend Yourself From Malicious People Using Dark Psychology and Manipulation Techniques

(Bypass Mind Control Brainwashing Tricks of Narcissists and Manipulators)

William Piaget

Published By **John Kembrey**

William Piaget

All Rights Reserved

Psychology Hacks: Defend Yourself From Malicious People Using Dark Psychology and Manipulation Techniques (Bypass Mind Control Brainwashing Tricks of Narcissists and Manipulators)

ISBN 978-1-77485-928-5

All rights reserved. No part of this guide may be reproduced in any form without permission in writing from the publisher except in the case of brief quotations embodied in critical articles or reviews.

Legal & Disclaimer

The information contained in this book is not designed to replace or take the place of any form of medicine or professional medical advice. The information in this book has been provided for educational and entertainment purposes only.

The information contained in this book has been compiled from sources deemed reliable, and it is accurate to the best of the Author's knowledge; however, the Author cannot guarantee its accuracy and validity and cannot be held liable for any errors or omissions. Changes are periodically made to this book. You must consult your doctor or get professional medical advice before using any of the suggested remedies, techniques, or information in this book.

Upon using the information contained in this book, you agree to hold harmless the Author from and against any damages, costs, and expenses, including any legal fees potentially resulting from the application of any of the information provided by this guide. This disclaimer applies to any damages or injury caused by the use and application, whether directly or indirectly, of any advice or information presented, whether for breach of contract, tort, negligence, personal injury, criminal intent, or under any other cause of action.

You agree to accept all risks of using the information presented inside this book. You need to consult a professional medical practitioner in order to ensure you are both able and healthy enough to participate in this program.

Table Of Contents

Introduction 1

Chapter 1: Foundations Of Dark Psychology 2

Chapter 2: Manipulation 8

Chapter 3: What Is The Difference Between Persuasion Or Manipulation? .. 24

Chapter 4: Dark Psychology And Persuasion 28

Chapter 5: "The Empath" 42

Chapter 6: Fraud 50

Chapter 7: Nlp Beginners 67

Chapter 8: Techniques Of Mental Manipulation 87

Chapter 9: Psychologically Manipulating Someone.. 94

Chapter 10: Hypnosis In Its Current State 106

Chapter 11: Fraud 126

Chapter 12: Manipulation And............. 138

Chapter 13: Undetected Mind Control. 149

Chapter 14: Normal And Dark Psychology Dark Psychology.................................... 159

Chapter 15: Techniques Of Dark Psychology, Tricks, And Secrets To Analyze People.. 176

Conclusion 182

Introduction

Do you want to make sure others share your opinions? Are you ready to live a more fulfilled life, get people buying something, and many other things? If you answered yes, then this guidebook is right for you.

We will discuss the benefits and how you can utilize manipulation.

This guidebook will give you information about dark psychology. It will help you to identify dark manipulators and stop them from using your advantage.

You can protect yourself against dark psychology by learning as much as possible about it. This book will teach you about the major types psychology that are subject to manipulation and darkness.

These chapters cover all you need to understand about mind control, manipulation, and more.

Chapter 1: Foundations Of Dark Psychology

Dark Psychology's core focus is on the darker sides of human existence. These include the study the pathologies that characterize human nature, the power to create meaning and form self-concepts using darkness, how to manipulate others, communicate with one's inner shadow and how transform oneself through confronting one's worst fears and desires by releasing tension (or climax), as well as other topics.

Dark Psychology isn't for everyone. Dark Psychology was developed to explore some of the most disturbing aspects of human behavior. As such, it's not recommended for those who are weak in heart. Dark Psychology is an interest that should not be dismissed.

Dark Psychology has many appeals. Some may be drawn to its taboo character, while others may desire to explore the demons within them, while others may seek to understand their human nature better.

Dark Psychology focuses primarily on the darkest and most taboo sides of human nature. It's a study of dark sides of humanity to understand and not suppress them. It addresses death and personal trauma as well as mental disorders and mental illness. Dark Psychology does not encourage the attainment these states of existence. They are still explored to understand their existence from an object-level (rather than an accusatory). The majority culture prefers to attribute human misery to someone else (e.g. a society or a person with a bad reputation). Dark Psychology, however, takes a more honest and objective approach to humanity by acknowledging that each of us is responsible for our misery. Dark Psychology investigates how we might use that knowledge to our benefit.

Dark Psychology is more interested than in what we as individuals are. Dark Psychology may not care as much about whether you are gay, straight, or both. Instead, Dark Psychology wants to learn why you are what you are, i.e. what your feelings are about your sexuality. Dark Psychology, on the other hand, asks about your soul.

Dark Psychology is a fundamental form of inquiry. It concerns the nature and place of you within the world. It addresses topics such as death, evil and sexuality. Dark Psychology is able to address all these topics within a single field of study. This is a departure from conventional psychology, which tends to focus on mental health and physical health.

Dark Psychology doesn't focus on the why' of an incident but rather on the how'. It is pragmatic in its approach to human nature, more concerned about practical outcomes than abstract inquiry. Dark Psychology isn't interested in finding out why people are so bad. Dark Psychology cares more about how we can make meaning out of this information.

While there are many ways you can practice Dark Psychology, the main ways are learning and doing. Also, while you may not be able to practice Dark Psychology directly, you can still learn about it through books and videos. Or you can engage in group discussions, or try your hand at it. Dark Psychology is not the same as practicing black magic, dark spirituality, or any other form of witchcraft. Dark Psychology is a practice that helps you change your consciousness through learning more about yourself, and/or relationships with others. Dark Psychology's primary goal is to help people see the darkness in their lives and understand it better. This can often require an individual to face parts of themselves that are difficult to accept or to deny. Dark Psychology is often considered to be a form self-psychology.

Dark Psychology, like other psychology, follows its own set of principles. These principles are meant as guidelines to help us better understand the human condition and change it. These principles include:

Dark Psychology begins with understanding that it deals with your subconscious's darkest aspects in order to transform them into something more useful. It's a hard practice that requires confronting your fears and neuroses as well as other issues related your self-concept. If you are able to explore the darkest sides of yourself, it will be easier for you to integrate them into your higher Self.

Dark Psychology doesn't have any boundaries. The possibilities that are available in Dark Psychology are endless. You may discover something dark in your own mind, but it may be quite the opposite for someone else.

Dark Psychology will require you to examine your darkest aspects. This means that you need to recognize the dark side of yourself, and then decide whether or not it is possible to change. It's best to avoid something you don't want to change. This will allow you to be at peace with the parts of yourself you refuse integration.

You must understand the reasons behind your darkness if you wish to transform your soul. It's important to not just accept it as a fact, but also to see it as part of a process. If you feel hatred towards someone or something, this could be due to a particular set or circumstances that you are not able or unwilling to confront. Sometimes it is necessary to confront the circumstances directly and face them head-on in order for hatred to be transformed.

Human minds are complex. They can bring up conflicting emotions. Dark Psychology's main goal is to help individuals understand their emotional conflicts and why they arise. You might be afraid of something that isn't necessary. This could indicate that there is an additional part of your mind that is afraid to deal effectively with your fear. It is much harder to integrate this secondary aspect if it is not obvious.

Chapter 2: Manipulation

Beginning our journey through dark psychological psychology, we'll start with manipulation. We will begin by reviewing what manipulation is. We will examine how you can understand the true meaning of manipulation. This chapter has some key goals. First, we will look at manipulation. The criteria for success will be discussed, then we will look at some common manipulation methods.

Manipulation is only evil if the end result is evil. Sometimes manipulation is necessary to obtain the right result. Sometimes you can't avoid it. You have to make the situation work for you. Sometimes it is necessary for someone to be manipulated to ensure that they are better off than they were.

What is Manipulation and how can it be used?

Manipulation refers to a form social influence, which is used for the sole purpose of creating certain perceptions and behaviors. In general manipulators will attempt deceive others in some manner. Their methods can vary from being almost invisible to being quite coercive. Executioners can be confused by some forms and wonder if the executioners are thinking too much or should they doubt themselves. Others, such as blackmail attempts or threats of violence, will be more explicit. There are many methods of manipulating people.

There is a reason for manipulation. It is used for controlling the other person. It is difficult to spot manipulation if you have ever been one. You may find yourself telling your self to stop reacting to something, even if it is completely justified.

Understanding that manipulation is powerful and can be used in a variety of ways is critical. It is essential to be able recognize common manipulation patterns so you can spot when someone is trying and control you.

It's important to influence others.

It is possible to make sure that you influence others successfully if you know what your doing. You can usually make it through it without anyone noticing. Be aware that manipulative behavior towards another person can cause you to be intruding on their mind. It is important to be open to the truth. You shouldn't manipulate anyone for any reason.

Criteria for Successful Manipulation

To manipulate successfully, you must meet three criteria. In order to avoid being caught, your actions must satisfy certain criteria. This will allow you to be sure the other person does not see you. It will also ensure that your actions achieve the desired effect.

Manipulation works like a perfectly balanced game. Everything must be carefully calculated and used in the right way to achieve success. These criteria include:

1. A willingness to deceive and hide one's true intentions

This allows the manipulator cover their desire to control another person. For them to be able to control the other person, they must conceal their actions. With a few key exceptions such as coercion and blackmail, if someone knows that a person has a tendency to manipulate, the chances of them succeeding are very slim. They must be willing hide their true motives so that the other person does not wait for the other to fall. If they are aware that you are trying control them, they will fail.

2. Awareness of the Vulnerabilities and Risks of Executioner

Everybody has their own weaknesses. You could find that someone is highly affected by others.

This could be a fear of negative emotions. Or they might have an inborn drive to please others. These flaws are the weak points in their armor, no matter how serious. They are the weakness manipulators must use to get what they want. If the manipulator plays their cards correctly, they will be able to exploit the vulnerabilities to get what they want.

3. A Certain Graduation of Ruthlessness

Manipulation does not come easy. And manipulators who lack the necessary ruthlessness will have a hard time getting the results they desire. They must be able to work with others to get the desired results. This means that they need to know what it takes. When they learn to control other people, it is clear that they ultimately have the power to achieve what they desire.

Manipulation techniques

Manipulation is one of the most complex strategies. These tactics can be tricky to master if one doesn't know how to do it. It can be extremely difficult to identify if you are on either side. Truth is, manipulation is done deliberately and carefully to retake power from the other person. Manipulators try to slowly intrude on the well-being or welfare of another person, until they can take full and complete control. They can then make sure they're the ones making the decisions.

You need to know how covert manipulation works. These steps are straightforward: The manipulator learns about the target, then gets close to them and ensures that they are not aware of any red flags or suspicious behavior. The manipulator is careful to treat the target as a friend, and not a foe. This position allows them to learn about the personality and actions of the other person. They want information about their targets and the best ways to control them. After that, they work with the manipulation strategy they accept and wait to see how they can make sure that the person is vulnerable and susceptible to the techniques of their choice.

They should achieve the desired result if they follow these steps: Someone who is so insecure with their position that they will be willing to defer to the manipulator because they have established a position of trust. We often hear about manipulation when we think of it from a relational perspective. People who seek to manipulate others will naturally approach people they trust to give them that control. They require trust and relationships to gain access and avoid detection. They often rely on the people around them to ensure that they succeed. This is so they can succeed.

There are many strategies that can be used to influence others. They may use different techniques, but the outcome is the same. They should masterfully control the other person to get the desired behavior.

Gaslighting

Gaslighting can be a common method of manipulating people. However, it is quite simple to do so as long as you have a good poker smile.

When lying to someone else, the key is for them to remain calm and convincing. If they manipulate someone they intend to make the other person feel inept or helpless. The manipulator may tell the other party they're wrong about something, even though they could be right. They make use of this tactic to try to control another party.

The goal is to instil doubt in the person and change their perception of reality. They will feel vulnerable or dependent on you for help when they don't believe the things they see.

This takes time and is done slowly. It can take several weeks depending on how deep they want to create this effect. If they have a good understanding of what they are doing, they should not be able stop at the surface. However, this requires mental focus and mental fortitude.

They generally start small. When a friend or partner mentions something, they need the other party to doubt it. The target could simply ask where the keys are, or go to the mailbox and check them out. When the target responds, the manipulator moves off to retrieve the keys. However, later that day, the manipulator mentions inanely that the keys actually were in a completely different room. This sets off doubt and is so innocuous, they probably won't argue about where their keys are or where they should be.

This slowly becomes a pattern over time. They may claim to have forgotten something and then hide it in the store. They might say that they took care a simple, unimportant task such as emptying the trash can. They might say that their target forgot to transfer the laundry to the dryer, or something similar.

Here, the idea is that gradually enough lies are shared that corrections to these errors become second-nature.

The manipulator doesn't make them think twice about it. Even if they do think twice they realize that they are wrong.

The manipulator might encourage the target's concern about their mental health to be expressed to the manipulator. By doing so, they create a situation in their favor. They can guide the other person towards whatever they desire. They can convince their target that they're wrong about most things and they will be convinced. After enough repetitions, the manipulator eventually reaches a point where they can claim that their executioner was completely wrong and unable comprehend everything.

Criticism

Another popular tactic is criticism. The manipulator can convince their target by criticizing the other side.

If the manipulator is able to recognize what they are doing, then their criticisms may be able to cut deep enough to cause enough doubt to the other party to allow them to use it in highly effective ways.

It matters greatly that you are able to do it. If the manipulator has these skills, they can remove the barriers between themselves and their targets.

Perhaps the most powerful shield against manipulation is self-esteem. It is usually the easiest to control those who have the lowest self-esteem. A manipulator can sometimes break down someone by criticizing them.

Imagine this: Someone just made their spouse a meal. The meal might not have been great, but the person who made it isn't necessarily the best at cooking. Perhaps the partner doesn't enjoy it as much as they would like or want the other to be better at it. They could be criticised by a skilled manipulator to get them to stop doing the same thing. They could tell them they're a failure if you can't cook properly or say they need to study more. They want others to see the benefits of their efforts and believe that they are making the necessary changes. They will make other people feel bad about their behavior until they make the positive changes they want.

People who feel criticized are more likely to seek out the approval of their critics, especially if the critics value them. They will do more to fulfill the criticisms they received because they know they could get some praise. They dislike being criticized. This makes them feel weak or incapable of doing anything.

Criticisms can cause a loss of self-esteem. People who have been repeatedly criticised by a loved one will lose control of their lives. The more they do this, they are more successful.

Redefining the Goalposts

Common tactics to control people include changing the goal that another person is trying to achieve every time they get too close to manipulators' desires. This allows them to move toward the desired action slowly, just like when you change your request for a dog to complete a complicated task. It's like training a dog for opening a fridge to get you a drink. Next, you will need to train your dog to open the doors. Next, grab the drink. Next, get the drink.

Although it can be a tedious process, this is exactly how dog trainers get their dogs doing what they want. The dog will learn each step by breaking down the larger action into smaller parts.

This is possible also with people. The goalposts are constantly changed.

Let's imagine that a manipulator wishes their partner to prepare them food in a certain manner every day at a set time. Their partner might start by telling them that they wish that their executioner was more skilled at cooking. The manipulator might then ask the executioner to learn to cook more and to adapt their cooking to fit his or her personal tastes.

Then they shift it even further and ask them for a time to prepare it. Finally they arrive at the expectation of having a meal every day at a specified time.

If they do it correctly, their partner will never notice the shifting of goals that slowly trains them to do what the manipulator wants.

The manipulator will most likely use emotions to manipulate the victim into believing that they have to comply with what is asked. As they become more comfortable with the task at hand, the manipulator realizes how much they will be willing to do it.

DARVO

DARVO stands in for:

Deny

Attack

Reverse

Victim

Offender

It basically means that a person will deny an accusation they've been made of and then turn it on the person who accused them. The victim attacks their executioner with an accusation. This will often put the victim on the defensive. While the accuser is trying to defend their accusation, the manipulator could reverse the roles.

This is a common tactic to control the other person. This is crucial in order to ensure that the manipulator can control the actions of the other person. If the manipulator wishes to control their executioner they will need them to be on other side.

If they follow these steps they can convince the other person that they are the problem. If they play their cards right they might be able control their executioner, even if the executioner makes a desperate attempt to deny it.

Imagine their partner confronting the other about their discomfort about something they did. They are then told that they are manipulative or abusive, and that everything is their fault. They will not allow those accusations to stand, especially if it is not something they did. They will spend their time defending themselves and trying prove that they don't manipulate. They stop talking about what really matters, the fact that their partner has betrayed them. The end result is that their partner does not have to confront them with the same problems and that they feel in control.

They then have to figure out how they can protect themselves.

Chapter 3: What Is The Difference Between Persuasion Or Manipulation?

Persuasion vs Manipulation

The key difference between manipulation and persuasive is how you try to persuade others. Persuasion may be used to promote positive things like a better product or service, or to persuade someone to change their mind. Contrary to manipulation, which is meant only to benefit one person.

Persuasion could be described as the most persuasive, rational and convincing way to present all points. Manipulation involves manipulating truths for one's ultimate goals. Persuasion is also a way to convince someone to do something they aren't interested in. Acceptable behavior can only be achieved if there is honesty and the right intentions behind it. One person may ask for a contractor's help earlier than expected, as they are unable to move in by a given date.

These arguments show that there is a clear intention. It would be possible to manipulate a builder by claiming that the wife has given birth or is in the process of giving birth. This is why there is a social stigma attached to deceit. People feel that they were coerced and lied to into believing certain facts. One difference is that people who are persuaded to believe another view are convinced that it is the best. All the arguments are presented and the individual is armed with the necessary information to support their decision. Coercion, a form or coercion that produces instant remorseful and compromise is called coercion. Because there aren't arguments, evidence of good intent or actual arguments being used, coercion is a form of coercion that results in instant remorse and compromise. The manipulator reaps these benefits.

What are the limitations?

Many people use the terms manipulation and persuasion interchangeably. They refer to the use and execution of processes in order to achieve a goal. They are associated with something cheap or poorly done by deceitful individuals such as dishonest traders who try and sell impossible things, ruthless politicians looking to reach the top, or other unscrupulous persons.

This is a false concept, as manipulation and persuasion can have very different meanings. They are used to describe situations that are different.

Both are dependent on convincing actions by one or several people. They are different because of their purpose. In our lives, we have all used persuasive and manipulative methods to communicate our ideas and goals. This could be to get approval from parents and employers, to get the attention of classmates at school or to pick the movie we want.

It all boils down a reason for doing what we do. Persuasion occurs when both the reasons behind these actions are positive and more so for those receiving the persuasive work. Both the persuader AND the persuader will be discussed.

But if the actions only benefit the person performing them, then manipulation can be described. The victim of manipulation is commonly referred as the manipulator.

Chapter 4: Dark Psychology And Persuasion

Persuasion within the dark psychology realm is essential for many purposes. There are many strategies that can be effective in different situations. As we discussed previously, observation and gathering information is an integral step that the practitioner uses to determine how to proceed based upon the needs of the patients.

After careful observation, your personality type will be known and you will be able create a plan that's most likely to work. This plan will take into account your intentions and who you need to assist you. These persuasion strategies can be used in many settings around the globe. Each situation is unique, but they are all applicable in different ways. Let's start discussing persuasion with Aristotle's Three Modes of Persuasion.

Ethos

Ethos is the first one of these modes. This mode demands that the speaker portrays a favorable character for his audience. Aristotle provides three prerequisites for preparation. They are competence and empathy. This sounds familiar? Let's start by focusing on competence.

You would expect that a salesperson or employee will know what you need and will be able and willing to explain it to your questions. It's frustrating to be asked a "expert" a question, and then get unsatisfactory replies that show this person doesn't know what they're talking about. If you are unable to make the product work for you or get an explanation, there is no way you will ever return to this store.

You can think of the scenario with the politician that we talked about earlier. One of the worst outcomes when someone makes an argument is when the speaker seems unintelligent. Or he might just be spewing out facts and figures which experts in the room know are false or fake. His credibility has been damaged immediately and it will prove difficult to rebuild himself, no matter how strong his platform. This is why the principle competence is so important in planning and execution of speeches or other approaches where an audience must agree with you on any subject. It's important that you know the topic you're speaking of. You shouldn't rely on your skills in making up new topics on the spot. It is possible to be too confident about your abilities, which can lead you to taking huge risks. If your audience realizes that you're just talking smoke, they will destroy the bridge.

Good intentions is the second aspect. People want to feel comfortable that you are on their side and that your intentions are genuine and sincere. This is difficult to communicate, so make sure you spend time learning about your background, and how you will present your argument. It could be that you want to convince your boss of a great company idea, or you might be trying to persuade voters to vote in an upcoming election. Even if the goal is to meet a young lady at a bar, it's important to recognize signs that you may not be who you seem to be. This takes practice, time, and practice. It is not possible to set out on your journey and achieve your goals immediately without having practiced with smaller-scale scenarios. Practice and planning are essential.

Doing your homework on this topic will help you to be prepared for any questions that might come up. You will be able to see and understand what people really care about.

This leads to the last tenet: empathy. When we are able to get enough food, water or shelter, our bodies crave the same thing. To get your audience to believe in what you're selling, it must be a positive feeling. If you cannot establish a connection in this area then you will have to resort to another method of persuasion. But, if you can build an empathic relationship, you will soon gain trust and relationships, which will make your job much easier in future.

All three of these facets create a solid character base which is the foundation of Ethos mode persuasion. Let's examine the second mode, Pathos.

Pathos

Pathos's method of persuasion focuses on the influence of emotion. In this mode, your first concern is to make the audience feel the emotions you want in relation to your argument. Let's examine an example.

A politician might tell a story about her painful childhood to get people's attention. She describes her childhood with an alcoholic father. He was a frequent abuser and left her family in dire straits. She believes that her father's alcoholism is the reason why she didn't have a good and healthy relationship with him. Because of this, she dedicated her time to building an organization to help rehabilitate alcoholics. She is speaking to potential investors and her ability to tap into emotions has resulted in several positive outcomes for her Pathos strategy.

The empathy portion of portraying strong characters in the Ethos mod, tapping into the emotions communicates that the speaker is genuine and honest with her intentions. It also shows compassion for other people who may be in similar situations to hers. This helps the audience overcome any doubt about her motives. If someone is trying to get money from you, it's important to verify that they will be using the money for the purpose they say they intend. Consider the street beggar, who tells stories about their lives to try and get some money. These stories may or might not be true but the intention is to make people feel sorry and give them money. While it is true that some people are forced to be out in the open, there is still a population who cannot avoid being seen. They won't stop people asking them for money but many people do so out of their own free will. But there are others who will not hesitate to take advantage of people's desire to help the less fortunate. They may tell stories about their life to get them to cash in a bit. It is important to remember that when people ask for information from people they don't know, they must establish a relationship with them. Pathos allows you to tap into universal human emotions and show people that your "likeness" is possible. People tend to gravitate towards those they find similar in fundamental ways. People are naturally afraid and hostile towards others. There is the internet that can tell us everything, right? Although you might be shaking your head, many people simply trust the beliefs of their parents or associates and are happy to do so. In these situations, it is necessary to convince a majority rather than focusing on the individual. It is possible that they will just return to their original beliefs based upon peer pressure and the influence of others.

Emotions are the best way to connect with others. However, people can be afraid of being hurt, so people often put up thick barriers to stop people from sharing their emotions. These people are difficult to crack when it comes to the Pathos mode. Perhaps Logos will be the third mode of persuasion that Aristotle uses.

Logos

Logos is the mode that appeals to people's logical reasoning. Ayn Rand's novels will be familiar to you. She is an example of how to present and organize arguments that almost only rely on logic. Her characters praise the virtues and benefits of reason in solving any problem and even building a perfect world.

However, it is not enough to just present facts to someone. There's a lot to know about how to organize information and present false information. It's possible to make a persuasive argument that isn't logically sound. Those who have studied logic will be able to tell you that it is a complex subject of study. To preserve the Logos style, however, our discussion will be limited to the creation and arrangement of an argument that appeals primarily to logic.

Logos believes that the persuasion technique is an alternative to those individuals with guarded feelings. This will bypass any hesitations that might be caused by past experiences.

The following is a typical arrangement for an argument: Since [fact 1] has been proven true, it follows that [fact 2) is also true. If it passes the logic test in the minds and ears of the listeners, then your argument has been successful. Remember that it is much more important for your target to believe what you say than to believe everything you have to say. However, the temporal component also plays an important role. If you want to have a long-lasting relationship, you need to consider the possibility you will be found out. This will also affect the amount of money you would be able to make. If you find out your target(s) finds out you lied, it will be a waste of effort.

When the interaction lasts only a few moments or minutes, you can convince listeners of a lot more. They won't be able to recall what happened until they are done with their task.

Think about the street magician. A street magician uses skills like sleight, to briefly convince the audience that something is occurring. The result is shock and amazement at the end, even though they realize very soon that they've been "tricked."

But, if you want to build trust with your target audience or establish long-term relationships with them, you need to present your researched facts in a way that persuades them to support you. Talking about news media sources and speeches or any other form of short- or long-form information dissemination is a common topic. We often discuss origins or text that favor a political party or belief. They provide facts and "spin", so you believe you have all of the relevant information. This is a common practice that engages all three modes mentioned in this chapter. Logos methodology can be tricky as you may not have a perfect argument. Instead, you need to present your argument in such a way that it seems ideal to your listeners. Your listeners will be impressed by your ability to organize your information in a way that rings true, regardless of whether it's true.

Techniques of persuasion, and the art of seduction

Your audience, the time you have, your agenda, and many others will all impact the art of persuasion. However, the study on human nature and how it works has produced a lot of valuable information that can be used across many different situations and personalities. Let's examine some common scenarios to show you how you can turn someone from an unknown person into a trusted friend in a matter of minutes.

You're at a party and want to approach an attractive lady in attendance. She is not an obvious target like the woman we showed in a previous example. Instead, she sits by herself and appears uncomfortable. This woman could be considered the prize for the "alpha" male in the room. She has charm and grace and is surrounded with interested men. We will refer to her as Nichole.

You arrive at the party knowing only a handful. You're not an unattractive guy, but you do dress well and are stylish. This isn't the only way to be able to command attention in a room and attract the love of a woman. You can quickly make yourself a household name and attract the people you love.

Here lies the key to your dilemma in this situation. Nearly everyone in this room will want to be entertained. If you can be an entertaining source for people, then power and influence will follow closely if you desire these things. Your first step should not be to approach the woman that you are interested in, as you will most likely be ignored or forgotten. The first step is to introduce yourself to everyone. Talk to the talkative people, share a joke with someone more intoxicated, and if they are hesitant to open up to you, tell them about your job or background. You might also be willing to give some of your information to win them over. You are an outgoing, confident figure that isn't too loud. However, you will silently take control of the room and conquer each person or small group. Some people will follow your conversations as you move and eventually you will catch the attention of someone near your target. If this is the case, you will approach the group in the same manner as others but may now be able to send subtle signals to Nichole that Nichole has captured your attention. Be subtle and not overbearing. As we have already discussed, the approach must be calm and non-aggressive. You are there for people to meet and have a great time. You don't want the appearance of a creep or someone who only wants to get married. You don't want to make it easy. This is a wonderful sign. Nice work.

The next chapter will focus on the one-on-1 interaction. We'll also discuss how to execute this step. Next, we'll discuss dark psychology and manipulation. Also, what is the difference between persuasion or manipulation?

Chapter 5: "The Empath"

Have you ever witnessed someone pick up the vibes in a room almost instantly? A person who walks into a room buzzing with excitement may immediately feel happy and energized by the people around them.

Or, they might just walk into a space and feel the tension hanging in the air immediately.

Have you ever seen someone pick up on the smallest details while watching another?

They are most likely the best person to people watch with because they seem intuitively to know what is happening in the mind of the other person at once.

It is possible to empathize if someone has mentioned this description to you, or another person. Empaths feel empathy in a way that is beyond the average capacity. Although empathy is something that most people experience to some degree, empaths feel the emotion more deeply than others. Empaths are able sense and often take on others' emotions. Being around someone in a bad state of mind can put an empath in trouble. Empaths are also affected by the pain of seeing someone hurt.

Before we go into detail about what an empath actually is, let's first examine the reasons for having it. Empathy can be defined as the ability to feel and understand another person's emotions, much like you are experiencing it.

Empathy is the reason you might weep when you see a sad film or read a story about someone who lost a child. It is why you may feel awful when you see someone homeless on the roadside or how you feel pride and accomplishment when your child meets a major milestone. It is the basis of all human interactions.

The basic purpose of such abilities is to aid in communication and in helping those within your inner group, which both help in the survival of the species.

Empathy allows people with empathy to instantly read the emotions of others. Your partner can clearly see that you are causing anger so you are told to stop and distance yourself.

You can tell that your child needs comfort.

A wider view may show you that someone in your area is hungry. If so, you may offer food to her. This will make her more likely than you to help her in the future, if she ever becomes hungry. This kind of selfless generosity builds bonds and creates communities where people help each other to ensure everyone is able to live.

The empath is able to recognize these traits but goes one step further. The empath feels more deeply the emotions of those around him or her. It is difficult for the empath to feel empathy when there is a close friend crying.

Empaths will help to soothe anger and hurt feelings. The empath can feel empowered to heal the hurting and lonely and will do everything possible to stop it.

However, the empath's selflessness and compassion make him or herself a unique individual. This makes them easy to manipulate. The empath feels the need to help others and is driven by his or her heart.

These feelings can be easily misinterpreted and turned into guilt. Expert manipulators may use these feelings against the empath to their advantage. The empath will try and understand and forgive the manipulator, simply because it wants to see the best of people.

Traits of an Empath

Empaths have many characteristics that are characteristic of them. These are the most frequent traits empaths display.

Sensitive

Empaths often hear one thing growing-up - "Stop Being So Sensitive!" But, this sensitivity may be their greatest asset. They are extremely sensitive to emotions and will stand by their loved ones. They are natural caregivers and will do whatever it takes to make others happy. They care deeply about others, and are sensitive enough to want to take care of them.

Introverted

The many struggles that introversion can cause are often a part of the human condition. The introverted empath often listens to and watches others and can become overwhelmed by emotions.

This can lead to the empath being vulnerable to manipulation from others, as they become disoriented and disconnected from all other things. This can often be accompanied by having to cope with conflict. Because the conflict is so difficult to manage, an introvert is more likely not to engage in conflict.

Intuitive

The empath has the ability to read and interpret what others are thinking and feeling. They are naturally in tune to emotions and can respond accordingly.

They can adapt their behavior and actions to the emotions of those around, to improve the mood and make the environment more pleasant for everyone. They want moods lightened and more pleasant because they are able to pick up on it and sometimes mirror it. But also because they truly want the people around them to be taken care of.

The Appeal of the Empath

Take a moment to reflect on the above traits and decide if the empath makes a good target for manipulation. The answer is yes, empaths are great targets. Even though empaths only desire comfort and peace, they are natural magnets for manipulators or energy vampires. They are toxic and exhausting people who just want to be around.

Because empaths are so in-tune emotionally with their surroundings, toxicity feels contagious. This effectively saps them of their strengths and makes it difficult for them to move on with their lives.

Empaths have a high level of empathy and are more likely to give all they can to those they care about. They are happy to see the people they care for brighten the environment. They find satisfaction in helping others through the compassion they bring along.

A skilled manipulator can make this into guilt, and use it to obtain exactly what he wants, even if an empath is unwilling to take part.

Since manipulators are aware that empaths can be conflict-avoidant, because of the drain it places on the empath, they may get away colloquially and legitimately murdering the other person if they are too scared to talk.

If the manipulator believes it is not worth the effort, the empath may not bring the manipulator to justice. Instead, the empath might continue silently to perform the desired task, using guilt appeals or other psychological tricks.

Empaths end up being the ultimate target for manipulators and other users of dark psychology. Because empaths are easy targets, manipulators seem to see some invisible marking that allows them to be spotted and engage.

If a manipulator doesn't make empaths feel guilty or enslaved by emotions, they will find it difficult to control them. The empath's emotions may be perceived by the manipulator to be their biggest weakness but they should instead be celebrated as a special form of strength.

It takes a special kind to have the ability to give unconditionally of one's feelings or show compassion.

Chapter 6: Fraud

The act of hiding the truth is called deception. It occurs when someone uses deceitful and illegal methods to get something or make people believe it is true.

Understanding Deception

You can deceive someone by making them believe something they don't believe is true. People will often claim they are not misleading other people even though they deliberately withhold certain information. Because they believe it will make it easier to trick them, many people do this. A simple question can be used to test if you are lying to someone. "If you aren't hiding anything, why not tell all the truth?"

You can ask yourself these questions to help you assess yourself and discover if your actions are causing harm to another person or misleading them. You can deceive others in many ways.

Your deceptive behavior can cause you to be narrow-minded, justifying it. This will allow you to do it without feeling guilty or held accountable. It helps people to have a narrow view on deception. This allows them to keep a positive image of themselves, which makes it easier to commit deception. It is important to withhold information in order not to deceive others.

It is not uncommon for someone you love to deceive you.

People are often hypocrites when it is about deceit. It's not wrong to give misleading or missing information. But, if it is you who are being deceived, you may feel deceived.

It doesn't matter what one thinks, deception is manipulative. One person lies to another in order to gain their selfish ends. A person who intentionally conceals the truth or misleads another to promote a belief is guilty of deception. This is a transgression when it comes to relationships and can cause a person to feel betrayed or break trust. It violates the rules of a partnership and adversely abuses expectations.

All people expect their friends, loved ones, and sometimes even strangers to be truthful. But, sometimes people use deceptive techniques without realizing how much damage they are causing. It is important that one avoids deceit if they want to maintain a good relationship with a friend, loved one, or loved one.

Psychology deceit

According to psychology, deception refers to the act or making someone believe something that isn't true. The goal may be cruel, kind, small, or large. The average person lies several times daily, mostly through little white lies. These lies are often excused by people who want to avoid unpleasant situations but never intended to cause injury.

The deceit does not have to be about telling others lies. It is not always about telling lies to others. People tell lies to themselves for many reasons. They start with small lies and then they become more serious delusions. Then they find themselves unable or unwilling to control them. Eventually, they manipulate themselves. These types of delusions are most often dangerous for the person.

Experts believe that self-deception can help a person. If a person believes they can achieve something, even when there isn't any evidence, it can be a benefit. This can be a motivator for the person to attain the goals.

Research has been done over the years to find out if someone is lying. The polygraph is the most commonly used method to determine whether someone is lying. Although controversial, it has been widely used in criminal cases to discover the truth. The polygraph does not detect deception perfectly.

Researchers claim that it is difficult to accurately measure individuals suffering from personality disorders such antisocial personality syndromes using a polygraph machine.

Why do people lie?

In reality, we all lie. We tell lies every day, even small ones that we don't consider harmful. Why do people lie? People don't like to be deceived. Public figures caught in lies can be a scandal that draws attention to their personal lives or even destroys their careers.

Detecting Deceit

It is not easy to detect deception. Many researchers have failed in their attempts to identify deception cues. One can deceive using a variety different cues. It is possible to increase your chances of catching the liar by identifying clusters of verbal and/or nonverbal dues. These cues will be identified against a set baseline which was established when a person didn't have to lie.

Deviations from the baseline indicate that there is a possibility of deception. But, this is not always true. It is possible to detect deception by comparing people's statements with some facts. But this method may not always prove effective. However, deception can be detected by many people using both verbal as well as nonverbal cues.

These are just a few of the nonverbal and verbal cues which could be used to indicate deception.

Lies tend to answer questions using other questions. Most liars won't answer a question directly. Instead, they will use another question for an answer.

To avoid being seen as unconfident about their communication, lying people avoid correcting themselves.

Many lies claim memory loss to cover up their inability to recall or recall certain facts.

The lieders prefer not to report what was done, but rather what was done.

The liars are always required to justify their actions, even if they do not need it.

Liars don't get emotional when accounting for events. To prove the contrary, liars prefer exact dates to reporting.

Most liars want a question repeated because they don't understand the answer.

Although most liars show emotions, they are often not real.

Most liars have few words to describe events and activities.

To deviate attention, Liars concentrate on the weaknesses and flaws in others.

Lies use passive language to describe things.

The opposite of a lying person is a truthful one. They tend to:

Refer to your past experiences and lessons.

They often refer to mistakes from their past when they are narrating an event.

They are open to dialog when someone is honest.

They do not use dates or timelines to report on different activities and events.

Truthful people will not sound fake or rehearsed when reporting on events and activities.

A person who is truthful will share information about unanticipated or unusual events.

To be truthful, someone may use sensory information such as how the place smelled or what it felt like.

You should be cautious when using any of the nonverbal and verbal cues above to detect deception. This is because there is no way to know if someone is telling the truth. Intentionally lying can also lead to people saying things that appear truthful. But, it is possible for a truthful person to come across as a liar. It is possible to detect lies, but it can be difficult.

Use deceptive tactics

Plays that are designed to deceive the opponent about their capabilities or intentions are called deceptive techniques. Someone using deceptive techniques wants their opponent to make the best decisions for the individual's interests. A person can make a mistake and still be able to make a good decision. When deception succeeds it decreases your opponent's options while increasing the possibilities for you. Some people are extremely calculated in life. They will deceive in an intentional way and think through the consequences before they do. This is called manipulation. To obtain their desired results, they will intentionally deceive their opponents.

So how can one trick another? In order to deceive others, you need to follow several steps. These steps are similar to those used by master deceivers:

Your goal should be clearly defined before you use any tactic or do anything. What are you looking to accomplish and what strategy is most effective to ensure your success? You want to create a situation that is unstable and gives you leverage. You may want to tempt your adversary by giving them a chance, or to make them think that they are the best at what their do.

Define your deception. A master deceiver can modify their strategies on the spot to avoid detection. They ensure their deception is convincing and simple. They have a list of what they want the opponent to believe. In some cases, simplicity may not appeal to your opponent's mind. Find a balance in what you believe and what your opponent believes.

Evaluate your opponent. They then sit back and plan how they will treat their opponent. They take into consideration the questions of their opponent and create possible answers that make the lie seem true. Deceivers are careful to observe their opponent and not what they would like them to be. This is vital if they are to succeed.

Synchronize information: You believe your opponent will agree to the deception. Now, a deceiver is going to continue selling the deception. Deceivers ensure that they have many options to conceal their deception. However it is always coordinated to avoid detection. People who use deception to manipulate are often careful about making sure the lies fall into place.

Keep your eyes open. Deceivers will alert you to the reaction of their opponent to their deception. They are eager to maintain the deception and change the narrative when necessary. The goal here is to maintain control of the game and ensure that the adversary does not notice anything that would cause them to do what the deceiver desires.

Business deception tactics

Negotiations are a common part of business. You can use deception in many different ways. It is used in business to gain leverage against investors, customers, competitors and opponents. There are many methods of deception used in business. These include:

Lies concerning the bottom figures, alternatives: If a counterpart is present at the table, they may bring a statement outlining how low or high they might go. This type of statement needs to be considered carefully and not taken at face value. Don't fall for the trap of believing everything you hear. Instead, look at the claims made and investigate other options before agreeing to them.

Even though they may seem great, some offers can be too good to resist. Avoid similar offers, especially when they come from a colleague. Most of these offers offer a poor deal. Take the time to review each offer and go through all terms. If you see hypothetical questions in the text, it's possible to tell if the deal is not right for you. A lot of offers are presented in abstract forms, which can often conceal some information. If in doubt, make sure to read the fine print.

The ability to escalate commitment: Sometimes it is possible for a person to agree to a large business commitment. You might be aware of the other party's desire for something similar, and they may not hesitate to offer you this opportunity. They can use your need to push to get you to hurry up with the threat that others may be looking for the exact same. You may make a huge investment in a product without thinking about it and be afraid of losing. It is okay to walk away. Remaining in the agreement you were duped into taking in the first instance will drain your finances more than walking away.

Absence of reciprocity. The norm of reciprocity states that concessions must occur on both sides during negotiations and must be done in equal measures. If your counterpart refuses to match your concession, or talks instead of showing commitment towards you, then avoid any further negotiations. Talk to them about your concerns and, if they don't agree, end the negotiations.

Last-minute nibbling. The request might sound small enough to convince you to accept it. To gain more leverage over you, a counterpart could use this opportunity to inform you that you must close the deal. It is important to be careful and insist that the counterpart makes similar concessions.

Fraud in Relationships

Trust is an essential part of a healthy relationship. Trust can be fragile. The relationship is at risk if the partners are secretive or use lies. We all lie. We tell small lies such as that we are fine, even though we are not, or that we like the gift you gave us. We also lie to people when we say that we don't have a romantic relationship. If someone was expecting us to send them a check, we would be able to lie about it being in the mail.

Honesty is vital in a partnership. Honesty goes beyond not lying. You can deceive anyone by making unclear or vague statements, lying, keeping information secret, telling half-truths and manipulating information to emphasize certain points. Because it can affect a relationship, deception also includes withholding feelings.

Most people consider themselves to be honest. The truth about a few people reveals our thoughts and feelings, especially when they are negative. You need courage to reveal your negative feelings or thoughts about someone close to you.

We can be exposed if we continue lying. Many people who lie are always afraid of being found out or being honest. This is why they lie more. Dark psychology is the act of lying to get your partner to do what you want. It can lead to harm in a relationship if there is deception. Some examples of deception that can cause harm are:

The deception can prevent you from having real intimacy with your spouse. A couple must be honest and trust each other in order to have intimacy.

Insincere acts can lead to deception and even more lies and omissions. It can become difficult to keep track. It can be more damaging to the relationship if the truth is out.

The truth can be kept secret for too many years, making it difficult to uncover it. If it is finally revealed, it can damage trust in the entire community.

The keeper of the secret is constantly weighed down with guilt and feels awkward during intimate moments with those they have deceived. Avoid certain topics and avoid closeness. Honesty can be a moral norm, but depending on the context or culture it might differ. Deceiving people is against religious and cultural norms. As a result, they feel anxious and guilty even though they are trying to conceal the truth. This is the reason electronic lie detectors use this type of physiological reaction.

A person's self-concept can be affected by how they feel about guilt. If a person lies for too long, it can affect their self-esteem. An individual feels guilt that was not handled honestly and it can lead to shame and a loss of dignity. Inflicting mental distress on the person who lies can cause deception. This could lead to health issues due to stress.

Chapter 7: Nlp Beginners

Let's start with basics.

Neuro-Linguistic Programming or NLP is a term to describe a successful way of developing self-confidence and communicating effectively. NLP is an efficient and effective technology to create change. This is what makes it different from other types or development disciplines.

What does the Name mean?

Let's look at the name briefly to help you understand the basics before we continue. "Neuro", stands for the mind and its influence on and control of the body. It is more than the physical brain. It is also the way that the mind affects the body at both conscious and unconscious levels.

The person's use of language (words, tone and questions) is known as "linguistic". Language can give you a glimpse into the thoughts of a person. By observing how they use language it is possible learn a lot more about them.

When the name isn't correctly defined, it can cause confusion.

NLP does not aim to program a person's thoughts, actions, or feelings. Instead, programming refers to the examination of patterns and thinking habits (their programs), and how they affect a person's life.

Each person has their program, but not everyone is aware of the impact they can have.

What is NLP?

NLP has existed for over 30 year, so it's not a passing trend. Its roots lie in the collaboration of John Grinder (Richard Bandler), and Gregory Bateson (Gary Bateson) in the early 1970s. Through observation and analysis, they were able to develop models of how the brain, language, and patterns that govern thinking create reality.

NLP developed from these humble beginnings to become a technique that can work in a variety situations. It is based upon behavior and observation to find life patterns and patterns that are working well. Once you have identified the patterns, you can strengthen and modify what works.

Pop Culture, or Valid Change?

NLP does not come without criticisms. Some argue that NLP is not a legitimate discipline as it has not been scientifically proven to be efficient. Others are more emotional and call it "new age silliness" or cultlike programming. These criticisms are valid to a degree. NLP cannot be empirically proved and there have been extreme instances of NLP being misused by practitioners to gain advantage of others.

NLP has value, even though there are extreme cases. These types of criticisms fail to recognize one thing: NLP is effective. NLP can be done by anyone with basic training. Many people have seen dramatic improvements in their lives through NLP strategies.

What makes NLP so powerful?

NLP is a simple and straightforward way to communicate with people and to develop oneself. NLP effectively addresses the structure of how people hold onto their realities. NLP provides the ability to immediately and intentionally change one's thoughts and behaviors by those who study it.

NLP effectiveness is directly affected by another critical element: practice. NLP techniques are best used when they are practiced and used frequently. NLP workshops and seminars are popular places to learn more. Participants can make real progress and grow when they put their learnings into practice in the real world.

NLP is an effective and popular method of personal growth. It is practical, behavior-based, and easy to use. Anyone who is familiar with the techniques can use them to enhance their lives.

A Comprehensive Guide To Neuro-Linguistic Programming.

Understanding how others behave is one of the most challenging aspects of life. Personal development is both a personal and professional aspect.

There are many ways you can gain more control over what you do. However, Neuro-Linguistic Programming is (N.L.P. The most effective and well-respected strategy to increase control over your actions is Neurolinguistic Programming (N.L.P.

This guide will provide information about N.L.P.'s history, core concept, and strategies. The benefits N.L.P. offers will be explained to you. Learn more about the many benefits that N.L.P.

The History Of NLP

John Grinder & Richard Bandler were the first to create NLP in 1970. The NLP was created by John Grinder and Richard Bandler, two Californians who drew from previous theories in the areas of psychotherapy, language, development and personal growth to develop their therapeutic approach to improving human behavior. N.L.P. contains parts that are deeply rooted in N.L.P. Parts and techniques of N.L.P.

Bandler & Grinder have been trying to understand human nature from an early age and how different brain parts interact with each other. The Structure of Magic I: A book describing language and Therapy was published by Bandler and Grunder in 1975. It became the basis of the system.

Bandler, Grinder, and others believed that language, our neurological processes, as well as our behavior, are all interconnected. Focusing on certain skills could help us use the connection to benefit from problems ranging in severity from phobias, to psychosomatic disorders.

The movement's early years saw the opportunity to use the growing literature about human potential and develop the idea.

Bandler and Grinder did not have training in psychology or therapeutic use methods. They felt this gave them the ability to create a paradigm shift.

How N.L.P. How N.L.P. was made commercially

This system was quickly popularized by the human potential movement at the close of the 1970s. N.L.P. had many positive aspects. N.L.P. were considered a helpful tool in personal development. The therapeutic benefits of N.L.P. were beginning to manifest outside of the immediate psychotherapy field.

The system was eventually commercialized and the methods were used in business. Bandler & Grinder moved beyond academic writing to start organizing seminars and events that would help others who wanted to learn more.

Around the N.L.P., there was a growing community of students and psychotherapists. This movement was quickly recognized worldwide. N.L.P. has been studied extensively by motivational speakers and self-help gurus. N.L.P. is used in teaching. Tony Robbins is one example.

Since then, opponents have claimed that the movement lacks scientific foundation. Yet, the movement continues to be widely studied and used in academic and informal circles.

N.L.P. It is used today for psychotherapeutic purposes. It is used in combination with Neurolinguistic Psychotherapy to provide a base for therapeutic disciplines.

Although the movement originated as a therapeutic approach, it is still being used in many other sectors. Due to the system's ability improve persuasion skills, negotiation skills, and sales, business has adopted aspects of it to benefit their industry. Many managers, business leaders, and coaches believe that the system offers many benefits for these people.

The Core Concept Of N.L.P.

Bandler's definitions for N.L.P. say that the system should be:

A model of interpersonal communication which focuses on relationships between successful patterns, and subjective experiences. patterns of thought) which are underlying them.

The idea behind this is that all people have the same basic neurology. It is how you control and manage your nervous system that will determine your ability to do all things in life. Furthermore, N.L.P. Your neurological system is directly tied to your linguistic patterns and behavioral patterns, according to N.L.P. All of them can be learned either through experience or programming. You can also take control of these aspects by modeling.

The idea is that your internal processing strategies can control external behavior. If you're making a sale for instance, your internal processing strategies are controlling the behavior. N.L.P. helps you to understand

and implement different strategies that can ultimately lead you to achieve specific goals.

For instance, if your goal is to improve social status, internal strategies can help you.

It is possible to also see the term neurolinguistic programming through each of these components.

Neuro is the neurological system. Our world is experienced through our senses. Sensory information is translated into thought processes, both conscious and unconscious. These thought patterns can impact our physiology, emotions, and behavior.

Linguistic refers primarily to the way language is used to make sense of the world. The words you use have a direct impact on how you experience the world.

Programming refers simply to the process and learning of things.

Three key components of N.L.P.

N.L.P.'s idea is easy to understand. The three core components of N.L.P. can be understood. These are learning, consciousness, subjectivity.

1) Subjectivity

Every individual experiences the world differently. As such, our subjective experiences can lead us to create subjective models of how things work. These experiences are constructed using our five senses and the language that is used.

These experiences are formed through the senses, of audition, tactition (olfaction), and gustation. They also come through the language we use for thinking and talking about them. N.L.P. argues that subjective experiences follow a pattern. It influences how you see, talk about, and act in the world.

These sense-based representations are responsible for controlling human behavior. The theory states that it is possible to modify the perceptions of the sense-based subjective experience to change the behavior.

2) Consciousness

N.L.P.'s fundamental premise is: The N.L.P. premise is that consciousness can be broken down into two distinct components, the conscious and unconscious. These unconscious representations may affect our conscious behavior, but we all experience them.

3) Learning

N.L.P. is also a third central concept. N.L.P., as you'll see later, considers learning the third central concept. Learning is a form of imitation, which they call modeling. The theory holds that imitative learn can reproduce any desired behavior and codify it.

The N.L.P. Communication model

These three core elements form a large part of N.L.P. theory and strategy. N.L.P. is another key idea. The N.L.P. is a communication model. N.L.P.'s communication model is briefly covered in the section above. The above section discusses N.L.P.'s view of human behavior, but here's a more detailed look at this guiding principle.

The N.L.P. According to the N.L.P. communication model, a person is always in a kind of behavioral loop. An individual's behavior outside creates an inner response. The person's internal response in turn causes them to respond in a specific way (external behavior). As you can see the external behavior causes an internal response.

N.L.P. was discussed previously. According to the N.L.P. system, external behavior is determined by the sensory experience. This includes visual, auditory (auditory), kinaesthetics, olfactory and gustatory. These senses influence how you behave internally and can cause you to learn further.

Additionally, your innate response to a particular external behaviour is a combination of internal processes. These are the different ways that you interpret the sensory experience. The internal process refers primarily to thoughts and sounds that are created within your mind. While the internal experience refers to feelings and emotions experienced.

N.L.P. Strategy of External and Internal Experiences

The N.L.P. Strategies deal with both external and inner experiences. Both these experiences result in a specific outcome. N.L.P. The N.L.P. strategy theory says that every sequence of events, both external and inner, leads to a particular result. It is possible to achieve a different result if you change the sequence or order of these experiences.

If you want to send an e mail, then you need to have a strategy that includes both external and internal experiences. It won't work if the sequence is changed or diverted.

The five senses that are involved in each strategy include the five senses of visual, auditory as well as kinaesthetic feelings, olfactory, gustatory and olfactory. The external behavior might be to send an email. This will create an internal experience of a specific smell or image, which can then cause you behave in a certain manner. These five sensory experiences may occur internally or externally.

N.L.P. therapist will focus on your internal experiences when you are in a meeting. For example, an N.L.P. will be able to focus on your internal and outer experiences. One example is how your eyes move when talking about a specific thing. These will help you understand your strategies better.

The T.O.T.E. The T.O.T.E.

Bandler, Grinder and others also discussed a T.O.T.E. Model. model. This refers to a model incorporating different N.L.P. Strategies, it is primarily used for explaining how a person processes information. T.O.T.E. T.O.T.E. is short for Test, Operate., Test, and End.

Bandler and Grinder are widely associated with the theory. However, the original concept was taken from a book written by Miller, Galanter and Pribram, Plans and the Structural of Behaviour.

T.O.T.E. The model is used to understand what triggers you to react in a particular way. The model helps you identify the factors that set a strategy in motion.

The test basically looks at the trigger which initiates the strategy. To verify that the process is complete, the trigger will continue to operate.

Consider it as motivating yourself for writing those emaileds. Consider the motivation that drives you to write. This would be the trigger. This is the trigger.

The next part of the model is the operation. Operation looks at both the internal and external processes that are required to allow the strategy for continuation. What are the responses from the outside and inside to the e mails?

Next, you'll perform another test. This test will show you if your trigger and operation caused the same strategy or behavior in the second test. If the test passes, which means that the behavior was similar, then the exit is possible. If you don't feel the trigger worked, or the experience was different, then you should consider whether it was wrong.

NLP has many benefits

NLP has been widely utilized in different industries. Its proponents believe it could have life-changing effects for most people. These are just a few of the many benefits that NLP offers.

Stress- and anxiety-reducing

NLP is one of the most effective therapeutic methods for anxiety. NLP has been shown to help those with claustrophobia who are scanned using MRIs.

NLP has a linguistic mechanism that can reduce stress and anxiety. Talking about anxiety issues can help people who are anxious feel less anxious. The guided sessions can give the individual a better idea of the situation, as well as strengthen the ability to react to stressful situations.

Enhance your business success

NLP can make a difference in your professional and personal life. You can become more productive and less likely to be slaving at the desk. Business success is possible when you learn to harness positive behavior and change bad habits.

NLP's primary focus is on learning and improving strategies to learn, which is crucial for business success. NLP helps you understand human behavior so you can reinforce your business's best business practices.

Creativity - Enhance

NLP strategies and techniques are also able to help you become more creative. Once you understand the effect of sensory elements on your behavior, it is possible to try out different ideas and strategies. This can help to see common issues in a new light.

Be free from fears or phobias

NLP can help you get rid of phobias and concerns. NLP can be used to modify your inner reaction when you see an animal or person you fear. Learn strategies to help you manage your emotions when you have to go public.

Improve your health, and strengthen your relationships

Although evidence isn't conclusive, NLP has been shown to improve mood and reduce depression. This is due to the fact that NLP strategies make it easier to replace unhealthy habits with better ones. The system won't have any adverse effects on your overall health so it is easy to find out if the system works well for you.

You can improve your relationships with people by understanding their behavior. Understanding how people work will help you understand and respond better to their negative views of life.

Chapter 8: Techniques Of Mental Manipulation

Dark Psychology has a key point: manipulation. Manipulation aims to alter the subject's perceptions and behavior. The manipulator uses many tactics to influence the subject's thinking about a particular thing, person, or situation. Manipulators can use different tactics, such as brainwashing and persuasion to convince others to follow them.

The layman must know the manipulations that each of us have had to deal with in our lives. The manipulator might be trying to benefit the subject or to hurt him. The downside to manipulation is that manipulators don't care much about the needs and feelings of the subject. Manipulators care little about the emotional or physical well-being of their subjects. They use blackmail, threats, and other methods to control people's minds.

Many times, subjects will recognize they are being manipulated, but not as a form of control or harm.

Some people see manipulation as a way to have a successful and happy life. In this sense, manipulators use a number of tricks and manipulations to overwhelm the subject. Some of these techniques/manipulations are as follows:

Lying

Manipulators may be involved in exaggerations, false stories or partial truths. They make the subject believe that they know the truth in order to get him to comply. For example, many brands make misleading statements about their product offerings that are not true.

Rotating The Truth

Manipulators alter facts to support their views. Politicians will often twist the truth to make their policy and rules more appealing. Manipulators using this strategy justify their statements through fake justifications, clarifications, and other tricks. They twist statements to support their views or ideas, even if they lack any original basis.

Withdrawal of Affection

People are often persuaded to give up their friendship and feelings for manipulators. Mental torture is used to make the subject comply. When one of the couples does not follow their lead, it can occur in a relationship. One partner may stop engaging in love, affection, or compliance with the other. The manipulator may ask the other to conform to his/her desired behavior.

Sarcastic Jokes

The influencer tells sarcastic jokes to his subject in front others to show how powerful he truly is. To show his power, the manipulator makes negative and mean comments towards the subject. The manipulator often wants people to refrain from making sarcastic and negative comments in front everyone.

Make Subject Feel Helpless

This type of manipulation often makes innocent people look guilty. Manipulators make the victim feel helpless for their poor lives. This stage is where the influenced believes that he's helpless and has no one to help him. At this stage, the influencer acts as a helper for the victim. The influencer seizes the helplessness of the victim and makes him follow his lead.

Use of Aggression

The manipulator uses aggression to demonstrate dominance and power over others. The manipulator will use anger and temper tantrums to intimidate the intended target. The individual becomes scared and focuses more on the manipulation's anger than the original issue.

Does the Victim Role

The manipulator at this stage swaps the part and acts as a victim to gain other people's sympathy. He makes contact with the intended victim, and gains his sympathy. The manipulator will automatically make the intended person follow his lead and satisfy his desires. This is the most common influence technique that pretenders use.

Pretending Ignorance

This tactic is used to hide the fact that the manipulator doesn't want to tell you what they want. The manipulator will pretend to ignore the individual. This is done to draw the attention of the person towards the manipulator. The manipulator will get the attention of the individual and he will oblige him.

Bedrohungs

Abusing and punishing other people is one of the most popular influencing strategies. Influencers are known to use threats and aggressive behavior towards their target. In order to force the individual into submission, the influencer often punishes him. The influencer can often use violence or mental abuse to punish the individual.

Emotional Blackmailing

To overpower an individual, the manipulator might use emotional blackmailing. The manipulator might try to manipulate the individual by making them feel selfish and uninterested in what's happening in the manipulator's life. This trick helps the influencer to better trap the individual, making him anxious and confused.

Pretending Empathy

People don't always empathize with manipulators or influencers. However, they may do so for their own benefit. They appear to love and sympathize with the person but in truth, they don't. This allows pretenders to incline individuals toward them. This is an excellent tactic to make someone follow you in a sound and calm way.

Positive Reinforcement

You know gifts and presents can be a sign to show love and charm. Gifts improve and change people's attitudes towards their givers. Positive reinforcement is a method that many people use. It involves the giving of money, favorite toys and other items. For example, parents might gift their child their favorite sports cars upon graduation. Teachers may gift their students with gifts for completing homework well.

Minimization

This tactic is used by manipulators to reduce their wrongdoings. Manipulators want to convince the victim that their actions aren't so harmful or damaging as they think. When an individual makes the manipulator face his wrong doings, the manipulator might view it as over-exaggeration and overreaction. To put it another way, minimization refers to the reduction of negative consequences of manipulator's wrongful acts.

Chapter 9: Psychologically Manipulating Someone

Are you open to the idea of using psychology in your daily interactions with others? A psychology degree is not necessary. You do not need to have the ability read people's minds. We can profit from social interactions between colleagues, mates and superiors by leveraging the situation.

When I use the term exploit, it doesn't mean that I am referring to someone in a negative manner. Manipulation might be beneficial. This could include convincing others to take a vacation, or going to great measures to get promoted. There are many ways to gain insight into the psychology of our experiences that will help us make better decisions.

1. Take advantage of the Body Language

The brain can instigate physical gestures and responses from everyday experiences. This type of action sends lots of messages to people around you. What does this all mean? This basically means you can read the body language of another person to find out what they can tell you, or manipulate them with nonverbal cues.

I'm certain you've heard that nonverbal contact accounts to 90% of communication (it actually is 93%). This means that so many of our interactions can go unnoticed simply because we ask for the promotion with our arms crossed, our eyes fixed on each other and our heads down.

It is as important to understand body language as to communicate it correctly. It will let you know if anyone agrees with you, is actively interested in what your doing, or thinks that you are crazy. Recognizing the differences in body language will allow you to improve your communication skills and spot potential dead ends.

Imitating expressions, postures, and motions can help to gain their approval or agreement. Interrogators can use body language as a way to assess fault. If you nod your head "yes" but mean "no", it could lead to you being incriminated. Our more complex communication means are gone, and we're reduced to animals. This is why it's important to use our subconscious contact.

Here are some interesting facts regarding body language

* Legoland employees cannot point. Instead, they use their open palms to build confidence. Instead they use up-facing hand signals to indicate direction.

* If you're having a good time with a group of people, the person you most trust is the one that you first make eye contact.

2. Change Your Perspective

Put a matrix on their minds to hide the truth. This one requires deception, tact, and, most importantly: rhetoric.

Are You Happy with Your Life?

Lifehack provides a solution to help you end your suffering and live your best life.

Take the Comprehensive Life Assessment.

We all do it every day. You can have a profound impact on how you see the world. It can also be affected how you describe the situation. Because it covers more than just what was said and how that was said, rhetoric is an important aspect of the definition. Tone and material are all used. Make sure to use rhetoric as persuasive as possible. If necessary, exaggerate and change the emphasis where appropriate.

Look at how you structure your points and how they relate to the emotions or reasoning of others. Do you present it as though you have an idea, or do you pretend to know? If you are unable to persuade someone to stop wasting paper for environment purposes, what can you do? Can you persuade them less paper means more work using a rational argument? If you are unable to see clearly, you can reframe a situation and make a more effective statement.

This will help to put things into perspective:

* Your mind will believe you slept well the night before, which is also known as "placebo-sleep"

* The Dunning Kruger Effect. Intelligent people underestimate themselves while illiterate think they are brilliant.

Studies have shown that the most common connection between your favorite song and a traumatic event in your life is your favorite song.

3. Learn from others

You can use people's psychological pressure points to your advantage. It could be a desire for acceptance, inclusion, or to fit in. Or it could be the polar opposite: a desire not to blend in and to swim against all the current. The risky decision-maker could be persuaded into making a bad decision. However, the silent crowd dweller might be prevented from doing something that would bring them out of the safety of the conformity.

Their weakness is your strength. Now all you have is to find out how to leverage it to your advantage. Are they prone to being overconfident? This could cause a stumblingblock. Is their self-consciousness about something that might be able to persuade? Kryptonite, the antidote to all kryptonite.

The more information you have about the psychological and thinking patterns of someone, the better you can control their emotions. To be successful in this situation, awareness is key. Understanding your pressure points like any other point is vital. Recognize your insecurities as well as flaws to build a solid defense.

Jim Sniechowski, psychologist, provides a detailed explanation of the principles and practices of emotional leverage. He also gives a positive view on the subject. He provides three simple guidelines for making the most of someone else's feelings against you.

* Recognize their emotional foundation. No matter how rationalized or rationalized their position, they still hold onto it.

* Understand that to make them move in your direction, it is important that you first determine their emotional value. Their sweet spot.

* Know your audience's emotional sweet spot and you can design an approach that suits them.

4. Remember the importance timing and opportunity

The jaguar has the ability to hunt professionally and strategically. Its ancestors' successes, failures and biological capacity to predict success are the key ingredients of its biological capacity to predict failure and success. It knows when it is time to strike hard and when it is time to put an end to its pursuit.

Move when it's right. This is what we are taught as children. Keep your eyes open for opportunities and stay alert. You might ask for favors, even if they are tired or preoccupied. This will make them less likely be irritable or to deny you.

Instead of trying to force opportunities, accept them and keep an eye out for new ones. If you are waiting to pitch your boss to the boss, don't force them to have a conversation. You may not get the chance to meet someone for weeks, but it is worth waiting. We can win or lose half of a fight when we meet someone with a strategy, depending on how they feel.

According to a recent analysis, judges are just as vulnerable as any other person to this idea, despite being our rational-thinking role models. The study revealed that parolees are significantly more likely (up to 65%) to be paroled earlier in the day than to be paroled immediately after a lunch break.

Endless possibilities

Psychology's miracles have no limits. It's a fascinating area to explore, but only if you are willing to put the effort to learn and use what you've learned.

Each of these variables has its own benefits. You can become a lie detector by learning kinesics (the analysis and interpretation of body language). If you don't pay attention to other people's tendencies or urges, don't care to show your circumstances to your advantage and don't notice the body language you use or that others send your direction, you're blinding yourself from a fascinating way of optimizing your exchanges in your life.

Dark Psychology: Mind Control & Manipulation

Dark psychology includes science and mind control. Dark psychologists refer to people who use fear coercion, persuasion, encouragement, and coercion to get what you want. Psychology, as it is known, studies human behaviours and focuses on thoughts, emotions, and beliefs. In this scenario, dark psychology would be a phenomenon where people use coercion manipulation, persuasion or motivation to get what their want.

Psychologists and criminologists invented the term "Dark Triad" for a simplified method of predicting illicit activity and problems in relationships.

These are the characteristics that make up The Dark Triad.

* Machiavellianism- The use and manipulation of deceit and deception to mislead people with no moral compass.

* Narcissism- This personality trait is characterised by a lack in empathy, grandiosity, egotism, and grandiosity.

* Psychopathy: Generally polite, attractive, but remorselessness is common.

While it's not something you want to do, many people are manipulated. The Dark Triad might not target you. Normal people, however, are exposed to dark psychology techniques constantly.

Here are some common techniques that people use:

1. Lying - Untrue stories or partial truths, exaggeration or untruths

2. Love flooding - This is affection, buttering a person in order to make a request, or compliments.

3. Withdrawal: Silent treatment, or avoiding one

4. Love denial – Withhold affection or attention

5. Reverse psychology - You can tell someone to do one thing to motivate them to try the opposite.

6. You restrict the choices you offer - This is when you give the person options that might distract from the one you would prefer.

7. Semantic manipulation is the use of words that appear to have a common definition. But the manipulator will eventually tell you that they have their own definition.

Even though dark psychology techniques can be used to exploit others for their ends, those using them are often aware of the consequences. Others may not realize that they are using immoral or dark tactics.

Many of them had learned these skills from their parents when young. Some learned these tactics by accident as they grew up or in their teens. They accidentally tried to manipulate people and it worked. They kept using the tactics to get their way.

Dark psychology is part of every day life. You'll see how easy it can be to fall for these techniques by reviewing the facts. Either victim or perpetrator, you can choose.

Chapter 10: Hypnosis In Its Current State

Hypnosis feels like when you go to sleep, get drunk, or dream. Every person experiences hypnosis differently. The experience is different for every person at different times. It is not a common symptom in hypnotized patients, but it can be noticed more often.

Like the other stages, a setting trance or settling is very important. The setting refers specifically to the way a person thinks and feels during a meeting.

Many people who attempted hypnosis have failed. They are mostly doing "stage hypnotism" to get attention from the media. You worry you'll lose control or do something stupid. Or worse, you won't feel like yourself. This is a mistake you made. In reality, you are always in control and the experience may be entirely different from what your fears were.

Today, people often have similar thoughts and convictions when receiving therapeutic

Hypnotherapy. This may not be the case for everyone. However, it is a good way to get a sense of what you might anticipate from hypnotherapy.

IT STARTS WITH RELAXATION

Relaxation, which is the state in which your mind and body are free from tension or fear, is a key aspect of hypnosis. Hypnosis doesn't calm the mind or body. Induction of hypnosis requires that your body and mind are free from any excess weight.

For instance, the hypnotist may help you to see how heavy your body is in certain areas. Hypnosis team members include the client and the Hypnotist. The client may feel ready and able to detect a sense loudness in the proposed body area. But, relaxation is your responsibility, and not that of therapists.

In contrast to the illustration ofhypnotics where the subject performs hypnotic commands and the recommendations of the Hypnotherapist are usually an invitation, not command. Consider the suggestions of the hypnotherapist and you might find it easy to forget all about your worries and relax. You don't have to follow any "must" or coercion during this procedure.

FOCUS ON WHAT IS IMPORTANT

Hypnosis requires that you focus. This is also the responsibility of the individual hypnotizing, and not the therapist.

Hypnotherapy usually takes place in a tranquil, isolated setting. People in this setting find it easy to relax and listen to the hypnotherapist.

Therapists are trained to guide your thinking in a way that can be helpful for dealing with addiction or suffering.

Before you begin, your therapist will go over what is expected of you. Your therapeutic goals and your hypnotherapist's aims have been discussed before.

The therapist will guide you through the process so that your attention can be on your addiction. Because you must be quiet and peaceful, the information that you need to focus on is often clear and simple. It isn't overwhelming.

OPEN YOUR MIND

Hypnosis attempts to create an environment that is more prone to addiction. The majority of people who receive hypnosis will think of reasons why the counselor's advice is not working. It could become a string of many "yes, buts".

People are usually more open to hypnose than when they are regularly awake and fully aware of the possibilities. Some people might become more aware and confident in their own abilities through this openness. The person is more aware of his potential than he ever thought possible.

This is because they don't have control over their actions. People under hypnosis are able to act in different ways than they normally would, but they do not usually do anything that goes against their values. Instead, we are able to see the possibilities before us and have a desire change how we look at things.

SENSORY MODE

Hypnosis, which is renowned for its unique sensory experiences, allows people to experience different feelings such as pain. Some people have had anesthesia-free surgery due to this. It can also cause changes in how you perceive and hear things.

These changes, as with all aspects of hypnosis can only be controlled by a hypnotherapist. One example is that the person's suffering has become more stressful. Many people discover that they are able to relax deeply and disconnect from pain. This can lead to separation.

SEPARATION

During hypnosis some people experience dissociation, or detachedness. It is often described as looking outside or like a person watching TV. However, those with hypnosis are able to see where they are and what their doing.

This sense of uniqueness may be described as an experience of hypnotic influence on an external perspective, or a feeling that you are able to see the world differently. Although some persons are not able to have an influence on the observer, it is evident to others. It can feel like someone is experiencing something out of body.

STAGES OF HYPNOSIS

Experts in medical and scientific fields have widely accepted Hypnosis as a safe and effective treatment that can make a difference in people's lives. If you desire to live a happier, more confident, healthier life, and to have less stress, you might consider Hypnosis.

Concentrating so intently on one thing, the hypnotic effect allows an individual to tap into the unlimited potential of their subconstious minds, allowing them to transcend perceived limitations and create physical and psychological change.

The process of hypnosis can be divided into several phases. We'll look at each individually.

INDUSTRIALS

How can a professional hypnotist relax a customer? How does a volunteer stage-hypnotizing perform during a complete event? Hypnotic induction is a technology that can be used in all cases.

This is the stage in which a person is hypnotized. The hypnotics/hypnotherapists can then employ several methods of profounding to guarantee that the topic is successfully hypnotized and follow their instructions throughout the session.

PROGRESSIVE HYPNOTIC INDUCTIONS

There are many types of induction. Some are quick, while others require only a few minutes. A "progressive Induction," also known by "progressive Relaxing Induction", is the most commonly used induction for both Hypnotherapy (and stage Hypnosis). As you might imagine, induction is slow and takes several phases.

The hypnotherapist will consult with his client to provide clear guidance. After that, he will ask him to continue his guidance. The hypnotherapist may offer many suggestions regarding gradual hypnotic rewards.

Breathing

"Take your focus off of your breath, and then relax more with each inhale.

Relaxation

"Let each muscle of your upper body relax slowly. The chest, abdomen, shoulders, arms and back. ..."

Relaxation and stress

You will need to keep your legs and hips tight. Now push your entire body into your feet. Now your whole body is ..." more relaxed.

Visualization

"Imagine you are in a tranquil spot... The perfect place to be... Observe how peaceful you feel. This beautiful place may allow you to just relax ...."

Counting

"I count, every number can you sink further into a trance... beginning at 10 ..."

These strategies are based solely on hypnotic suggestions being used and approved. Some clients may respond better to the physical suggestions. Others may respond more to visual ideas. While others might prefer to think more abstractly and use more mental and cognitive strategies.

These are just a few of the many aspects of gradual hypnotic stimulation. These are the most common and most accepted because most misconceptions about hypnotism have been dispelled.

It's possible to believe that it is easy to do a gradual hypnotic inducement. It basically involves asking the customer to do something, and then simply indicating it. Hypnotic inductions can involve more than simply speaking to the customer.

EYE-FIXATION INDUCTION

Another method of hypnotic Induction is "eye fixation". The therapist tells the client to look deeply into his eyes, just like a light or an image. This technique works by making the client focus on the image while getting tired. This is when the hypnotist uses his voice to offer suggestions or manipulations.

The therapist orders the customer close his eyes and to fall into a trance.

FAST INDUCTIONS

Another type of induction is called "Rapid Induction". It is usually indicative of a quick process, as the name suggests. They are often used by hypnotists as they seem dramatic. These techniques have become more popular in recent years.

Induction that is quick is very effective to keep induction short and to allow the therapist to get into the therapeutic part for longer periods. Rapid hypnotic Inductions work best in conjunction with clients. If there is significant discomfort and you only have a few moments to work, it may be a better option to use a more relaxing, longer-lasting technique. There are three kinds of quick hypnotic stimulation:

Induced Shock

Shock induction is when a therapist gives a client an immediate command, such as a jolt of "sleep", to do anything. This prompts the client into a trance-like state. It is easier for clients to sleep than to try to comprehend the cause of the jolt or how to respond to it.

We know it is the same hypnosis that we use for sleeping. We know. The term induction shock is used, and hypnosis has been often associated with movies and literature.

Inductions into confusion

Confusion is similar in nature to rapid, hypnotic induced shock. It is designed to make the customer feel overcharged and unfocused. You could ask them to count 10,000 in springs at 37, while they shake hands and sing their favorite song. (Deceptive sound?)

They will be confused and overwhelmed if you include them in multiple activities. Additionally, sleeping is more effective than trying to follow bizarre directions.

Induction of pattern disruption

This hypnotic inducement is used to prevent hand-shakes or other contact. The goal is to interrupt a subconscious routine. This is because the customer's subconscious routine will be disrupted and their mind will be confused. Then you will let them go to sleep or into a trance.

CONVERSATIONAL-HYPNOTIC INDUCTIONS

Some hypnotherapists do not prefer to use a formal intro and prefer to participate in "talking therapy." The same effects can be achieved using conversational techniques of hypnosis. But it's indirect and hidden.

It is a way to communicate with the client about a topic that is not related to his treatment. Here is a good example of dialogue-induction.

Thank you so much for being here today. Thank you. It was wonderful to see that you relaxed even though we had just sat down. Many people claim that they can almost enter hypnosis once they sit down. Perhaps it's because of the way you feel when you lie down on my couch. I wonder if you'll slip into a state of trance. Hypnosis is something we can talk about for a while before we go into hypnosis. We would not want to introduce you to hypnosis before your are ready.

A lot of hypnotherapists will use these techniques in hypnotherapy courses. Pre-hypnosis prepares the consumer for further introduction. Others use these techniques in their entirety without the need for formal hypnotic introduction. Many clients see the process beginning and want to know.

DEEPENER

Deepening, which is the most common approach to hypnotic induction, is probably the best. This is an effective way to facilitate a seamless transition that allows for more success in recommending the best possible treatment.

We must clarify several hypnosis issues, especially during the deepening phases, as we investigate further. Many people feel that they are "deep" in hypnosis. They believe this to be an indication that the hypnotizer has all authority and can even make suggestions that would be against their character.

The common misunderstanding stems from hypnosis allusions in pop culture, films, stage and stage hypnoticism, as well as hypnosis allusions to pop music, which frequently use the tropes for dramatic reasons. You won't lose your memories due to hypnose "deep", or the hypnotic being in total control of you or your body.

Hypnotherapists are fond of using the term "deephypnosis" often. If the subject is in a state of openness and receptivity, the expert will be able to offer his ideas. The more trance-like the customer is, the more it will be open to changing. Therapists use deeper techniques to help clients get out of trance quickly and make them more responsive.

Induction is usually followed by hypnotic depthening. It may occur at any time during the session. It is not required to use hypnotherapy, but most hypnosis providers use deepeners so that clients are open to receiving further treatment. This is how it looks.

After a client has gone through the induction procedure, the hypnotherapist may decide that the client will experience a deeper hypnotic state. The most common type of deepening is called the "staircase". The hypnotist guides the customer through a mental image of himself climbing down a step. To give the client a clear mental picture, they often start with a detailed description.

The therapist could also count down from 20 to 20, but it doesn't matter what number. At every stage, the client is motivated to relax and feel more relaxed. They are in a calm, comfortable state when they reach the base of the stairs.

The hypnotherapist counts how many stairs they have and gives well-thought out suggestions for increasing relaxation or dismissal. Once they reach the bottom, their deepening will be complete. The therapist might choose the next phase from this point.

The depth of hypnotic trance can be deepened in several ways. Because they are most well-suited to therapeutics and relaxation, hypnotherapists tend not to feel stressed. One such method of relaxation is the staircase deeperener.

There are many options, including the method of fractions in which clients are led into a trance-like state of relaxation. This could include a gradual relaxation, as well as the practice of yoga or advancement.

The stage hypnotist, on the other hand might be more eager to surprise his viewers or volunteers. Instead of relaxing, they might use a shocking or surprising induction. They also keep the relaxing deepeners away from their patients since they are not performing for dramatic purposes.

MOST COMMON TYPES OF DEEPENING

There are many options for deepening hypnotism. Here are the top ten.

Deepeners Numerical

All of them can be used as numerical deepeners. You can number up or you can count down. You count down. This counts allows the mind to alter and allow for deepening to occur. To make the process even more profound, the statistics can be supplemented with common suggestions like 'deeper and deeper' and 'deeper slumber'.

Deepening Natural Phenomena

The most common natural result of the hypnotic deeplying process is to reassemble the limb to normal after an induction or levitation of the arm. An example of a pure depth phanomenon is when the customer exhales in order to get the physical simultaneous indications he breathes.

Deepeners for visual involvement

This is where the individual is encouraged and supported to focus on an image or concept within their body, often a vacation destination or other desired location. This helps to create distance from the surrounding environment and makes it easier to reach out for therapeutic help, such relaxation.

Deepeners in dissociation

These are all important developments that promote isolation or the separation of an individual from his/her present time/space. Many people claim that dissociation, which is the core of hypnosis and serves all that supports it, is the key to hypnosis. The most common method of deepening detachment involves the individual moving from the body. This can lead easily to deeper visual participation, like a visit in a special place.

Deepeners triggered, conditioned

They differ from other types deepeners in that they are slightly different. It wasn't intended to be deepening when it was presented at first. It signals for deepening, instead. The word triggered could refer to "sleep", "relaxation", "now," or any other suggestive term.

The reference phrase is used to bring the person back into the same condition as the reference sentence. In this regard, the hypnotherapist may appear to be in deep trances before the reference word is installed. If the trance gets too deep, or the hypnotherapist feels the need to increase the depth of the trance, the expansion phrases can be used.

Chapter 11: Fraud

Do you know when your friends and family are deceiving? You may want to know how others deceive you for your own benefit or be able identify when someone is trying deceived you. Deception is a useful skill that can be learned regardless of the reason you are interested. It is possible to understand deception so that you can defend yourself against its grasp. This will allow you to avoid it happening, simply because you know what to do and how to prevent it.

You should avoid deceit if you wish to maintain your ethical standards. However, sometimes deception can work in your favor. A deceiving skill could prove helpful if you're ever in such a situation. It is possible for certain professions to learn this skill just because it can prove useful. There are many methods to deceive. Understanding all of them can help you be more successful.

Definition of Deception

First, you have to understand how deceit works. It is a psychological phenomenon that involves someone trying to trick another person. It is a deliberate attempt to trick others through words, actions or behavior. Although it is sometimes ethically permissible, such as when clinical trials are being conducted to detect biases, it should be avoided if necessary.

The purpose of deception is, ultimately, to mislead people or promote untrue beliefs. There are many ways that this can happen. Some people will claim that certain types deception are more honest than others. This could be justified by praising some while loathing others. Deception could be considered fraud. It can be punished by criminal law depending upon the severity.

Types and Uses of Deception

There are many methods that you could use to deceive other people. There are many deceptive methods and ways you can trick others. You can lie, or omit specific facts. Both are active forms of deception. Anything intended to alter or misrepresent truth counts as deception. This section will provide examples and a list six of the most popular types of deception.

The Truth About Lies

Lies are perhaps the most popular way to deceive other people. Lying involves giving false information to the other person in order give them misleading information. Imagine you have to go out to a party but you would prefer to stay home or do something alone.

Knowing that your friend, who is also the guest of honor, will be crushed, you create a lie that allows for you to go. While you might claim that your stomach is rumbling and you are afraid of making others sick, this excuse may not be convincing to the other person.

There are two main types of lying. The first is lying by commission. It involves adding false information to what you're saying. This is the most dishonest type of lying and it is in its purest form. Lying through omission on the other hand means that you leave out information. If you lie by omission you won't give any information you don't know to be relevant.

Equivocations

Equivocations may involve indirect answers, or ambiguity. You are basically trying to conceal the truth by using equivocation. This is often used in politics to hide truths or avoid being unpopular. It can also serve as a tool in court. Lawyers will recommend that the person who is taking the stand uses ambiguous, equivocal terminology to avoid the individual admitting guilt but also not lying. It conceals the truth behind ambiguity. This allows for plausible deniability.

Imagine a politician talking to you about the effects of a new taxes on everyone. When asked how much each group would be paying, the politician said that the upper income bracket is paying more than the lower income. However, this is not true for their discretionary income. It is not clear whether the politician meant the lower class would pay a lower disposable income percentage or overall.

Concealments

Sometimes people will leave out certain information in order to conceal the truth. People will tell only parts of something that are relevant or good, and leave out the ones that they feel are harmful to their goal. In order to avoid answering the exact question, they might answer indirectly.

Imagine your coworker asking you if he's stolen anything from your desk. He might look at your desk in shock and disgust, before saying loudly, "Do you look like someone who would take?" He did not answer directly the question but implied an answer. Many people will believe that they are not lying, even though they avoided telling the truth. Although not necessarily lying it is an attempt to conceal the truth.

Exaggerations

Exaggerating is a way to stretch the truth. The exaggeration becomes deceitful at some point. If the exaggeration is used to boast or boost your own worth or importance to the extent that it can be seen in a false advertisement of oneself, it's often considered deceptive. It is also possible to be deceptive by exaggerating in an attempt to induce sympathy. As in the case of the child who runs to the adult in control during a fight and then makes herself look miserable while blaming others for starting it.

To avoid being held responsible, exaggerate injury, discomforts, or pain. Deceptive exaggerations are different from innocent exaggerations. You don't want to be seen as lying. It is easy to make people believe you are exaggerating inadvertently.

Understatements

Contrary to exaggerations some people understate. That is, they reduce the reality to make it easier to accept. If you understate something, it can be used to convince others that the situation is not as severe as they may think. It can be used innocently to convey politeness, modesty, humor, or comedy. Or it can be used to deceive others and misinterpret the truth.

Consider that you are babysitting. Your child is running around in circles and leaves behind a large goose egg on their forehead. It looks like he has a dark eye. You could send a text message to your child's parents informing them that your child has been hurt. However, you don't want the parents to worry about the child. The child is fine, with the exception of the obvious bruising. When they get back, they will see that it was a minor bump. But, you were able care for the child for as long as they needed.

Simulation

In simulation you deliberately present things falsely. You can either distract or fabricate your way to this effect. Each of these techniques is intended to deceive the other. For example fabrication is the act of making someone appear to be someone or something they are not. In an attempt to convince authority, you could present yourself as an expert on a topic. You might also pretend to hold a license or qualification you don't. On the other hand, distraction allows you to distract another person from the truth by giving them something that might or may not be true. If someone wants to prevent someone from finding out that their degree was falsified, they might instead offer up another credential in order to distract the other person.

Recognizing Deception

Once you've learned the most common deceptive techniques, you're ready to recognize when deception occurs. Not only should you be looking for the strategies mentioned, but you should also be looking for other signs. Even those with a good understanding of deception are often caught unawares. The following steps can help you identify deceivers in your own life or those you suspect are trying to deceive. If you are trying to determine what their normal behavior is, then use this information to search for signs of stress. Pay attention to body language and vocabulary. And listen to the voice.

Take a picture showing the baseline of each individual

First, it is important to understand the neutral body of that person. There are some people who are naturally anxious. You do not want to make assumptions about their natural body language and think they might be lying or deceiving you. Because people are different and will naturally position their bodies differently, it is important to get to know the person neutrally. Try to have a normal conversation and ask questions that you would never lie about to get an idea of that person's neutral body language. In interviews, you can ask the person about their hobbies.

To get a better idea of her nervousness or deceitfulness, you can also ask questions about her age, date of birth and other similar questions.

Look for unique stress signals

After creating a baseline you can compare, you can start to recognize if the person lies to you. As lying is often very stressful for the body, you should be looking out for signs of stress. You may notice a rise in heart rate or breathing rate. However, you may not be capable of detecting the increase. The presence of self-soothing behaviors like biting or touching the lips, touching the skin, or playing with jewelry may cause your heart rate to increase. If these behavior patterns aren't present before, it is possible that they are lying to you. Sometimes, the person might freeze up for a few seconds after you ask something. This flash of fight-flight response is a sign they are telling the truth even though it lasts only a brief moment.

Pay attention to your body language

Remember the Body Language List that you were given in Chapter 2? To make sure you're familiar with all the common cues, now is a good opportunity to review it. The most common signs of deception are listed below. There is also a list that uses nonverbal language which, when combined, almost always implies lying or dishonesty. There are four parts.

Touching hands: An individual might touch their hands frequently, or may play with a watch or a wedding ring to disguise this behavior.

Touching the Face: The person who touches the face, especially the eyes and mouth, is signaling that they want to hide something.

Arms crossed: Crossing arms creates a barrier between the individual and the other.

Leaning Back: This allows for some distance between the person and the other person. It is desirable during periods of dishonesty.

If you observe all four of these behavior patterns, there's a good chance that they are lying. While this is not an exact science. It is impossible to look at someone without knowing that they are lying. However, this group of body language signals is sufficient to make it worthwhile to start looking for more signs of lying.

Listen to word choices

Listen to how they are phrasing the information and search for deceit. Understanding how they are done will help you be more alert to the signs of deceit.

Pay attention and pay attention to pitch.

People with stress tend to have higher pitches. This is because when people are stressed out, their voice tends to be louder. These people might also drink more water to help dry their mouths. This is also due to the same tension and stress which tightened the vocal chords.

Chapter 12: Manipulation And

Conversational Hypnosis

What is Hypnosis and How Does It Work?

Hypnosis can be described as a psychological technique which involves inducing a state whereby the individual loses the ability to make voluntary decisions. In hypnosis, a person loses touch and focus with the physical world. The act of visualization is used to create a new world/environment within the mind. Talking to others in another world can be heard by a person. People who are hypnotized respond well to directions and suggestions. People can use hypnosis for therapy to heal from various ailments.

Hypnosis is an old practice, but it is still controversial. Although psychologists may suggest that people who are in hypnosis do not have control over their actions or thoughts, others claim they can still exercise free will.

Hypnosis is either induced or natural. Natural hypnosis is achieved without the individual asking. Psychologists believe that adults must experience hypnosis at minimum once per day. Below are some examples of hypnotic state. With this in mind, you cannot use a hypnotic condition that occurs naturally to control your mind or actions. It is possible to control your mind by inducing hypnotic states.

Music is one of the best ways to induce hypnotism in someone. Playing music that is between 45 and 72 beats per minute will likely transport the mind into a hypnotic mode. Such music can have a transformative effect on the thoughts and ideas of an individual. Because the music plays in the same time as your heartbeat, it is synchronized with your heartbeat. The music's beat perfectly syncs with your brain, so every song has a perfect beat.

You can also use guided hypnosis to induce hypnosis. Guided hypnosis takes place at the table of a therapist and is the most common form. Hypnosis is the only type of hypnosis that a hypnotist can perform. Hypnotists lead people through a visual journey which can transform how they think.

Hypnosis employs guided relaxation and intense focus to create a state known as trance. This state of mind can cause the person's attention to be so focused on their phone that they are unable to see or perceive anything. You may have seen someone walking on the street with their mind fixed on their phone until they almost get hit. This is a person who is in hypnosis. In hypnosis, you don't feel the world around. Everything is focused only on the world you have created inside your head. For everyday life to begin again, you have to let yourself return to the real world. Hypnosis has two characteristics:

Suggestion therapy - A person is taught to respond to suggestions through suggestive therapy. When a hypnotist does hypnosis on an individual, the person only pays attention to the direction given by the practitioner. The use of hypnosis can be used to help people change their habits like quitting smoking and nail biting.

Analysis: Hypnosis can be used by an experienced hypnotist to achieve a new result. Hypnotists can help people relax and extract valuable information. This analysis helps the therapist identify the root cause behind mental or social disorders.

How Hypnosis Workes

Hypnosis works when the person who is hypnotized wishes to be suggested. It is a state of mind in which the hypnotist carefully guides the client through their mind to help them discover what they want. You will see that hypnosis is a means for two people to come together and make something happen. If you are able do this well, it is possible to help the other person achieve great results. Hypnosis is often used to assist people in accomplishing things they didn't know they could do. Common one is helping people lose weight. First, convince your mind that you want to lose weight. Some people struggle with this and never lose weight. With hypnosis, it is possible to make this happen.

Hypnosis works as it allows you access your unconscious thought processes later. This is exactly how NLP works. It is possible to encourage your mind by telling your unconscious thoughts that you must change them and then actually doing it.

Think about this for a second: you want to lose some weight. Your subconscious mind is convinced that you will fail. Perhaps you have had failures in the past. Or maybe you believe you are too weak-willed and incapable of making it happen. Whatever the reason, it is likely that you believe that weight loss will be impossible because you think you are the problem. Then, what do YOU think will happen? It is obvious that if your belief system doesn't support the idea of losing weight, then you will not be able. You are setting yourself up for failure and have already defeated yourself. You have become stuck.

But, you can get into hypnosis to change your subconscious and unconsciously thought patterns. Instead of telling you that you cannot lose weight, you can remind yourself that you can. All you need is persistence. It is possible to fix this problem.

Now that your subconscious mind has been redirected in another direction, your subconscious will be more comfortable trusting you and your thoughts. You'll be able take the time to lose weight because your subconscious mind will believe that it is possible.

As you can see, NLP is essentially hypnosis. It's a partnership between two people that alters the thought processes and results in behavior change. When you do this, you will be able to alter your behaviors quickly. Both NLP, hypnosis and other methods can influence the mind. These powerful forms can both be used in different ways but all have the same end goal.

Hypnosis: What to Do?

It is safe for performers and athletes to be in hypnotism, but it can also pose a danger. Your suggestionability is 25% higher when you are in guided hypnosis (or music-inducedhypnosis). This means you will accept others' suggestions easily and may do things that are contrary to your wishes. It is important to be cautious when you let someone perform hypnosis for you. You should not let anyone lead you to hypnosis, unless they are trusted professionals. You must immediately stop communicating with someone who is trying to manipulate your mind into hypnosis. You can easily get trapped in hypnosis if you allow others to make these moves around your body.

How to Make Use Of Hypnosis

You can use many techniques to hypnotize someone undercover while you are conversing with them. These techniques can help you put someone in to a hypnotic stupor. Once you are in hypnotic trance, it is possible to give commands to your subject. They will obey if they are suggested.

The pattern interrupt is the earliest form of hypnosis. Human beings are very similar to computers. A computer might fall into a "loop" if it comes across bad coding or an unexpected command. Our brains enjoy familiar patterns or rituals and are more likely to get confused if they run into something that is not expected. In this state, the person becomes vulnerable to all commands. The following is an example of how to conduct pattern interrupts: When someone holds out their hand for you to give them a handshake. Instead of reaching out and taking their hand, put your palm flat against their chest. This will confuse you and give you a few seconds for commands.

The second covert method of hypnosis is not very similar to hypnosis. It's quite nontheatrical, but it's incredibly powerful. The "imagine method" is a way to get your partner to think about the possibilities. You might find that your communicative partner believes they have made up their minds after you use the imagine technique.

The Zeigarnik Effect is a hypnotic technique. This technique can be compared to a pattern interupt because both are only useful if they create confusion for your communicative partner, even if it's temporary. The Zeigarnik Effect posits that the human mind longs for completeness. If something is not done properly, the mind will get stuck. However, it can be mentally completed if there are no other tasks. The subject's mind may become stuck if the subject isn't paying attention. However, the hypnotist could give them commands or insert suggestions in their subconscious mind. To test the effect, tell your friend a fascinating, detailed story. The story should be stopped at the middle. You can then start to give suggestions or commands to the subject during the silence.

The confusion caused puts the subject in a trance like state.

You can even put a partner into a full-blown unconscious trance, without ever touching them. This is very similar to stage-hypnotism. Begin by approaching the person that you would like to have hypnotized and engaging them in conversation. The conversation should be lively for a few seconds before you start to yawn, telling your communicative companion how tired. Watch their behaviour from now on. Keep telling them how tired and you will see their sleepiness increase. After they become quite tired, you can whisper the "sleep" command. You can use this command by saying, "Keep feeling the same once you're asleep." The communicative person should then fall unconscious. Make sure you catch them. If they are in this state, you should make them very suggestible. Simply command them to get up and go.

However, hypnotizing can be done by anyone. You can hypnotize others, too. Self-hypnosis may be useful if you have lost weight or stopped smoking. It is easiest to hypnotize oneself by lying down, or sitting comfortably, and closing your eyes. Once you've closed your eyes, begin to focus on the top of your head until it is clear what its dimensions and weight are. Do the same for your neck, shoulders and head. Continue working your way down until your toes are covered. Once your body is fully conscious, you can enter a state of hypnosis. When you're in hypnotic, you can give yourself instructions (e.g., "I will quit smoking"), and you'll find it easier for you to follow those commands once you return to your normal state.

Chapter 13: Undetected Mind Control

Your mind is your sanctuary. You are the only one who can see your mind, so you don't have to worry about what others might think. Or so we think. People like to believe they can control their thoughts and actions. Our minds can easily be influenced by others. If we don't pay attention, others can control our minds.

Imagine a time when you were watching a horror movie. Your emotions and thoughts are already being influenced and led by the film. Every decision made by the director, including the camera shot and lighting, will affect how you feel about and react to it. The prompts will be interpreted by your brain even though you are fully aware that the movie is being watched. How powerful would the influence of a dark manipulator if our brain could be so influenced?

Mind control that isn't detected is often the most deadly type of mind-control. Someone who is already conscious of the influence on their mind can make a physical, verbal, or mental objection. For example, they may choose to have no contact with the person in control. Many people will run when they notice a dangerous person trying get into the brain and take control. However, if the mind control can access the brain of the victim without detection, then the victim is not allowed to defend themselves.

To take control of the victim's thoughts without detection, the manipulator has two options. It involves using media and interpersonal interactions. The only exception to this was a larger company. The interpersonal interactions were the sole responsibility of the mind controllers. However, technology has made this obsolete.

Individual manipulators can now use smartphones and laptops to exercise media mind control. It can be used by manipulators as a powerful tool. Undiscovered mind controllers can still use many of these methods. However, they tend to be more deliberate than others and will only make their decisions after careful consideration. They are often viewed as more cowardly that other controllers such as psychological manipulators. Yet, they will do anything to find a suitable victim.

Undetected Mind Control Tactics

Now that we have learned a bit about undetected mind controlling, it is time for us to look at some of the techniques used by manipulators to control victim's mind in an obscure way. We will examine both the media and the interpersonal methods in the manipulator's arsenal. Let's now look at some of those undetected mind-control tactics.

Finding those in Need

First, you need to find someone who is pursuing a goal. It has been shown that people who feel satisfied and at ease are more susceptible to mind control. It could be as simple as someone wanting to drink or thirsty. It can also be psychological, like someone looking for affection or love.

The experiment to study subliminal influences and undetected control of mind is a great example. The film was shown to two groups of people, and the film contained an image of iced coffee. The first group was thirsty, while the second wasn't.

After the movie, the participants were given the opportunity to choose from a range of drinks. It was clear that those who were thirsty would purchase more iced tea than those who didn't. It is clear that brains will happily accept suggestions as to what they should buy when they feel desperate.

What would it look like to use this principle on a more interpersonal basis with someone? The mind controller will be able find a victim that is already craving something, and the manipulator can then control the victim more easily. For example, a victim may be in a breakup and want to control them. They might want the company back again and the mind-controller would influence their victim to believe they are the victim's savior. They will do harm to the victim and even cause them financial ruin, but the victim may fall prey to mind control.

A manipulator will exploit many needs of their victim. These include their need to be surrounded by others, their need to belong and their need to have financial stability. For many reasons, someone with more experience will influence these vulnerabilities. They may be looking to exploit victims financially and sexually. They might seek to gain victim's cooperation in order to form a cult. Some manipulators do this for the pleasure of their victims.

Be Restrictive

Restricting choice is another method of undetected mindcontrol. This form of mind control can be subtle as it provides the manipulator with a number of built-in "getout clauses" to protect the victim from becoming suspicious. This form of mind control will take away any choices the victim may make in a given situation while giving the illusion the victim has complete control.

Let's imagine that a woman is asked out on a date. A regular guy will spend time asking the question before stumbling out an open-ended one. It could be, "Would I like to go on a date with you?" The woman can answer this question by saying yes or no according to their preferences. This is how people who aren't manipulating other people will behave.

However, someone trying to control their mind will approach everything differently. They will use their charm to charm the victim confidently and effortlessly. They will make that victim smile and lower their guard. The manipulator will then ask the victim, with great confidence and assurance, "So, would you like me to take you out on Thursday?" It restricts the victim's choices. Because the victim doesn't have an option, they will select one of the dates provided. The victim can't claim that they weren't in control but the manipulator had total control.

If the victim is caught by the manipulator, or they realize that their choices are limited, the manipulator can make a backtrack, but still seem innocent. You could say to your victim, "I can't believe how much you're analyzing me words." That hurts my feelings and makes it hard for me to speak up." It can also make the victim feel resentful and weak, which could lead them to give in.

Media Control using Images

Like our five senses, our enemies can also be our guides. Our sense of sight can be very powerful. Visualization is a powerful tool that allows us to visualize our dreams, even when other senses are impaired. This can make imagery, as well as visual manipulation, a powerful tool to control media mind.

Due to technological advancements, manipulators around the world have access to impactful imagery techniques. They can even adapt these techniques for their particular victims. Consider a victim who seems to be afraid or averse to certain things. In such cases, the manipulator might use the feared imagery to access and then warp the victim's emotions.

Let's see how this type mind control could work. Today's world is filled with smartphones, videos, and many other things. Every video is shot in high resolution and can be sent to others at high speeds. A high-tech manipulator could use this to create the image. Consider a boyfriend manipulative who knows his girlfriend has a fear of insects. In such a case, they might "accidentally" place a book with a photograph of an insect on its cover somewhere during their video chat. The girlfriend will not be consciously aware that the book is there but she will sense the effect on an emotional level.

Media Mind Control using Sound

To control mind, the manipulator can also use sound. However, experiments and personal experience confirm this. Do you remember a song getting stuck in your head? How difficult was it to get that song from your head? Even though the song was familiar to you, the effect it had on you may be significant.

Undiscovered audio manipulation has a greater impact. Experiments have shown that wine orders from certain countries are more likely to be placed if customers are exposed music from one region. It was only later that they realized the influence of music on their decision-making.

Although you can see examples of the media mind-control with sound in the media and the government, individual manipulators can also use this type. Subliminally controlling the victim's sleep is one of these mind-control techniques. A skilled mind control specialist can find their victim when they feel most vulnerable. This is when they can insert dark and devious commands into the victim's ear. It allows the power to reach the very bottom of the victim's brain.

Another form of auditory control is to disguise the words using words or sounds that are similar. This is a form of mind control that affects people outside of their normal perceptions. These sounds will have a particular frequency. It is possible for them to cause fear, anxiety, or panic in the uninitiated. Once the victim feels scared and trapped, the manipulator is able to take control of their situation and do what they wish.

The manipulator has many options for mind control to use on their victim. The victim and the manipulator's goal at the time will influence which method they choose. The most important thing is that manipulators must be able to mind control their victim without worrying about if the victim will learn. All of these factors can work together to ensure the manipulator gets what they want. Often, the victim won't even know what's happening until it's too much later.

Chapter 14: Normal And Dark Psychology
Dark Psychology

Dark psychology is the study on why some people are really evil. However, dark psychology is more concerned with understanding how and why certain people prey. It assumes that every person has dark impulses. Humans can easily imagine themselves being mean to other people or manipulating them emotionally to do what they want. If we get angry, for example, we may say things like "I just want the kill them" or even "I'm so mad that I want to hit them." But most of us don't actually do those things. We suppress our emotions and don't take any action. We know that abuse of others and mistreating people is wrong. Dark psychology is an attempt to understand others who don't look like us. This includes those who behave on their worst urges and cheat, lie, and manipulate in order to get what or believe they deserve.

This is in sharp contrast to positive psychology, which studies how certain qualities and practices can help a person live a happy and successful life. All of the actions and behaviors associated with dark psychology can be traced back at the fundamental drive in all human beings to prioritize their goals and desires over other people. Dr. Michael Nuccitelli is a psychologist and forensic expert who pioneered the concept of dark psychology. He wanted to understand how humans prey on other people's thoughts. Dark psychology holds that some predators are guilty of atrocious acts for money, sex, or another purpose, while others do it without any purpose. They do not want to harm anyone or feel powerful, but they just want it.

These concepts should be considered before we dive deeper into dark psychology. First, there is the "dark range." The most manipulative and callous behaviours exist somewhere along this spectrum. These types of behavior can be anything from a minor nuisance to others to causing death and harm to them. The "dark factors" are the places where one's actions can be categorized along the dark continuum. Every person has one, but not all people have the same. A person's dark factors are the result of their life experiences, genetics, personality, and other factors. One example is if someone is raised in an abusive environment and learns that harming others is acceptable. The "dark sole" is the mental place that allows a person to do horrible acts without a purpose. The dark singularity, which is an area of someone's mind that seeks out to hurt others for its own ends, is called the dark singularity. The dark singularity is a dark element that can be found at the very end of the dark spectrum. It is impossible to reach. However, psychopaths who are extreme, like murderers and criminals, will unconsciously seek this place. Because all behavior is a function of some kind, it is impossible for anyone to attain it. Hurting someone simply to feel strong still indicates that there is a purpose behind the offensive actions.

Combining the dark continuum, the dark factor and the dark singularity gives rise to the dark singularity. There are many factors that can hinder or aid someone's journey to the dark singularity. The destructive person tries to attain the dark singularity all the time, but never succeeds. Take the dark continuum (whose dark factors can be affected by outside conditions), and you will see how close someone gets to the darkness singularity. Below is a brief overview of what dark psychology might look like in your everyday life. Did you ever meet someone who poured their heart out on you, even though they didn't know you? This kind of person will show their love by constantly reminding you of how committed they are to you, with gifts and compliments. They then show their true selves. As soon as they disagree with you or have reason to doubt your reciprocity they will turn on them. They might be rude or call you selfish. This is love bombing. It works because showering someone with affection will make them more committed and more likely to get involved with you. There is no way to leave this person. Once you feel trapped, the abusive person's true self can emerge. Their manipulative, possessive, or downright nasty nature will be revealed.

Another tactic that you may have experienced is the choice restriction. The choice restriction is when someone gives you options that will distract you away from the decision they want. The manipulator may restrict your choices by speaking favorably on one option and disregarding or making negative remarks about the other. While all three options are valid, the manipulator is seeking a specific outcome. To get their victim to follow his or her lead, he or she will distort the information about each option.

You might also have been a victim of covert emotional manipulation (CEM), or may have even done it. CEM is an approach where the manipulator manipulates someone using subtle cues and actions. This may include silent treatment and guilt-tripping. CEM leads victims to be more dependent on the manipulator and to question their own abilities. The victim may begin to doubt themselves or have low self-esteem over time. They might also do everything they can in order to please the manipulator.

Dark psychology is the science and art of evil, cruelty and callousness. It is well worth learning. Understanding the worst people will help you protect yourself. We may not be able empathy with those who try to harm us. It may be possible to avoid manipulative or cruel people by knowing the signs.

All humans can learn a lot from the people who are most evil. The psychopaths who suffer from Antisocial Personality Disorder (ASPD) can offer valuable insight into our responses to stressors as well as the mechanisms that lead to some people becoming incredibly cruel. ASPD can be viewed as having two major parts. One piece is a personality without remorse or empathy, with little emotional depth, callousness and a lack in care and regard for others. Antisocial behavior is another piece of this personality disorder. Antisocial behaviors include poor impulse control, uncontrolled anger and irresponsibility. ASPD personality and emotional traits seem highly heritable. This means that it is more likely that someone close to you, such as a parent, will display these traits. High levels of personality traits that are associated with this disorder are a reliable predictor of the behavior described.

These facts are just a few of the many that you may be surprised by. ASPD personality traits may be highly inheritable, but the behaviors are not. The other way around is that being cruel to your parents does not automatically make you a cruel person. Antisocial behaviors do not just depend on genetics. They are also influenced by other factors, such as poverty, trauma, and delinquent friends. However, these risk factors do not necessarily precede any antisocial personality characteristics a child might have. Psychopaths have traits and behaviors that are genetically determined, combined with antisocial environments.

What does this all tell us about ourselves? This antisocial personality disorder can help us understand how evil and darkness can consume anyone. If a parent has mistreated them and they develop the disorder, it's not their choice. However, adults may choose to surround themselves with people who bring out worst in them, even if they never get a full-blown personality disorder.

Terminology

Dark singularity is: According to dark psychology there is an area in the human mind that permits atrocious acts between people. This is the dark singularity.

Dark continuum. Again, dark psychology says that we humans have a pool of malicious intent towards other people. This can include anything from innocuous acts to outright deviant and psychotic behavior.

Dark factor. There may be some accelerants that you should consider when you are approaching the dark singularity. This is the dark continuum. It is the combination of these accelerants and the dark nature of an individual.

Dark triad. In dark psychology, this consists of the personality characteristics of narcissism. Psychopathy. Machiavellianism. They have evil qualities, as we've already mentioned.

Characteristics of Negative Personality Traits

These individuals are not the ordinary types, and oftentimes, they tend to confuse even psychologists--thanks to their high scores on measures of callousness--which is described as the lack of empathy for others. They tend to be emotionally flat, and they are often not remorseful. They believe and behave as though the world should work for them and manipulate others around them with fake emotions and high level deception. Additionally, they are social and outgoing, which may surprise some who don't know the dark side to human nature. These people are often extroverted and easy-going. This allows them to make good first impressions. This serves as a platform for future cruel acts that will make the lives of their victims miserable. But there are clear differences between these groups, which can have implications for the extent of harm and damage they can cause to co-workers and those with whom they are in close relationships.

In clinical psychology and law enforcement, research on the dark trio has been done. It was found that those who have high levels of these traits are more likely be to cause social distress, create serious problems within organizations, and even commit crimes. Although they may have different characteristics, some of their characteristics share certain common traits.

Identifying the Dark Triad's Traits

Psychologists used to distinguish the above traits by measuring each personality type separately. Peter Jonason was an assistant psychology professor at University of Western Florida. He and Gregory Webster also created a rating system called the dirty dozen. This scale measures dark triad traits by using a 12-item system. It asks individuals questions they answer.

The test gives the chance to score anywhere between 12 and 84 points. The more a person scores, the greater their likelihood of developing dark triad tendencies.

Research has proven that the dark trinity's three personalities are all aggressive and only care about their own personal gain. They can manipulate and exploit people by using various techniques and may violate moral values and social norms. It is possible that these personalities could be caused by genetic factors. Machiavellianism, psychopathy, and other personality traits are more closely connected because they both display malicious behavior. The vulnerability and defense of narcissists is a bit more evident. This is because their arrogance is often a cover-up of deeper feelings that they are insecure. Research also shows that men and women have more dark triad personalities. This may be due to the fact that men are more susceptible to these traits or because of social norms that allow them to be above the line.

None of the three personality types is honest or humble. Study after study has shown that cheaters of all types are less likely to be caught when they realize the risks. Psychopaths and Machiavellians lie to cheat when their energy levels are low. However, narcissists have a different approach because their dishonesty is not intentional but self-deception.

Relationship between the Dark Triad and Big 5 Personality Test

The Big 5 personality assessment measures extraversion and agreeableness. Many people mistakenly consider agreeableness to mean charm and charisma. It is more towards trustworthiness. Compliance, kindness, humility, modesty, and selflessness, all of which are positive attributes that promote good relationships. Machiavellians as well as psychopaths tend to lack in conscientiousness. Psychopaths often have the lowest level neuroticism. It is the inability to experience negative emotions. This is what makes them even more sinister. Narcissists who are the most calm of the 3 members of the triad and the most open-minded, are more extroverted than the rest. They are creative because they are more open.

Origins of the Dark Triad

It can be difficult to trace the roots of the dark trio. Researchers are however looking at these possible causes to find out:

Nature vs. nurture

Biological origins

Evolutionary

Researchers attempt to determine how genes and environment affect personalities. This is where twin studies come in handy. These twin studies can be described as follows:

Researchers can compare the personality traits between identical twins and fraternal siblings, which means they share the same environment. Fraternal twins are more likely to share half of the genes that identical twins do. However, fraternal twins tend to share around 50% of the same genes. In order to assist with such studies it is possible for researchers to conduct twin studies. They can determine the genetic influence of identical twins by subtracting fraternal twin relationships and obtain the correlation. The genetic influence is represented by the 50% difference in these twin studies. You need to double this number in order to achieve the full (100%) genetic impact. This is called the heritability index.

The genetic component of the traits has been determined to be biologically inherited. Researchers have found that individual gene differences drive relationships among members of the dark triad. Machiavellianism does not have the same heritability as the first 2 on the spectrum, but narcissism is more common than psychopathy.

Surprisingly though, environment seems not to play a role in the development of negative personality traits. Even though this influence is not as subtle as it used to be, it is still significant. Machiavellianism seems to be more susceptible to experience than other dark traits. This claim is logical because there is less variation attributable to genetics with this trait. It is more likely that the natural factors are responsible for this trait.

The evolutionary theory may also be used as a way to explain the dark triad characteristics. Evolutionary behavior is a factor in the development of dark-triad personalities. It may even be encouraged. People with dark triad traits may seem to be quite successful. Unfortunately, success with dark triad traits is rarely sustainable. These traits place emphasis on motherhood and mating. This strategy is fast if it focuses on mating. It's slow-reproductive when it focuses on parenting. Some of these dark traits may be related to fast life strategies. However, others are not. Researchers are still trying out to find more definitive results about evolution's influence on the dark trio.

Here are some interesting facts

Science has shown that people with darker personalities are judged to be more attractive, especially after their first encounter. This shouldn't surprise you. The truth is that dark triad people tend to be more focused on their appearance. The difference in appearance and attractiveness between dark triad personalities and others is likely to disappear when they are dressed with simple clothing and no makeup. This is the most common triad of dark triads.

The dark trio is also connected to honesty-humility. The HEXACO personality scale measures the honesty-humility factor. It measures aspects like modesty and fairness as well as greed avoidance, sincerity, sincerity, scepticism, and fairness. Like the big 5 personality tests, honesty-humility was found to be negatively associated with dark triad personalities. This is because these traits often exploit others for their gain, while the personality model reflects the opposite.

Chapter 15: Techniques Of Dark Psychology, Tricks, And Secrets To Analyze People

Why Analyze People

Different people have different ways of analysing people. You may choose to analyze people because you want to understand them. To establish an authentic connection with another person's mind, you must have an inbuilt way to understand them.

For a moment, imagine that you are trying get a deal for a client. It is clear that this deal is important if you are to keep your job, and maybe even get promoted. But you also realize that it will be hard to manage. The best way to understand the thoughts and feelings of someone else is to be able read them.

Consider this: You will be in a position to determine whether the client is comfortable and then respond accordingly. It will help you to determine if the client is lying to you or withholding information. It's possible to discern if your client is not interested, feels threatened, or annoyed by your attempts at influence. You can then determine how to reply.

If you are able to understand another's perspective, you can control your behavior. To ensure that your persuasiveness is guaranteed, you can tweak your behavior. Your behavior can be adjusted to make your client feel more comfortable.

In many other situations, it is important to read other people in order to not only be able and self-regulatory. By being able read by another person, you can guard yourself against any dangers that might arise. Reading someone else's position will help you understand it better. You can learn how to persuade, manipulate or manipulate another person. You can convince people to do what they don't normally do.

Analyzing other people is so beneficial that it is well worth the effort. This skill allows you to feel more connected to your emotions and can be used to make claims about your emotional intelligence. You will be able self-reflect and identify your emotions, as well as learn to watch your body. It is important to understand people in all situations.

How to analyze people

Although it may sound daunting, understanding how other people behave is not nearly as difficult than it appears. There are no complex rules you have to memorize, or skills you need. All you have to do to understand the behavior patterns and what they mean. Once you've identified the behaviors you can usually begin to identify their intent.

It's possible to begin to understand what the narrowing of someone's pupils means and then to match it with other actions or behaviors. When someone's body language is not consistent, it can be difficult to tell what they are trying to convey. People are often unaware of the workings of body language, and it is easy to find crucial information from it when they interact with you.

This helps us understand people. It is well-known that thoughts, feelings, or behaviors can be linked. Your thoughts are what create your emotions. The feelings you experience can also influence your behavior.

This is usually an unconscious cycle. It's not something you are aware of. Many therapy schools, like cognitive-behavioral psychological psychology, recognize this cycle and have begun to use it. This cycle is there for you to recognize. You can then use your knowledge to reverse the process.

In other words, you will be looking for the behavior of others and then trying to trace it back to the emotions behind them. This is why it is so important to be able to read body language. If you can see the motivations behind someone's behavior you can begin to understand their feelings. If you are able to understand someone's feelings, you can start to discover the underlying thoughts they have. This is probably the closest thing to mindreading that you can achieve.

There is a simple way to analyze the behavior of other people. First, you need to determine their neutral baseline. This is their default behavior. Next, you need to start looking for deviations from that neutral behavior. You then need to begin to examine the interactions of several behaviors in order to determine what is happening inside someone else's mind. This process is easy. This is a simple process that can be learned and then used to communicate with others.

Establish a Neutral Baseline Behavior Set

Understanding how to identify someone's baseline behavior is key to understanding them. This will enable you to effectively analyze the behavior of the person in a neutral context. This will enable you to determine what the individual's peculiarities might be.

Someone who is reserved or especially shy may exhibit several common signs and symptoms of discomfort. They may put their arms across their chest to protect themselves, or they might stand up and avoid eye contact. This is a common sign of lying that you'll see later in the reading. But a shy person won't lie if they refuse to make eyecontact and cross arms.

Because everyone is different in their personality and other peculiarities, this is an essential first step. A lack of this information could lead to you believing that anyone shy might be trying trick you. It is essential to have a clear picture of the basic personality and nonverbal communication styles.

Conclusion

Dark Psychology plays more of a role in our daily lives than most people realize. It affects us daily. It can happen at home, at work, or at school. Every day, people attempt to manipulate us - changing our thought and feeling.

All humans are prey to dark manipulators. We all are susceptible. You can learn how you can protect yourself by understanding their motivations and methods. It is possible to use this knowledge to manipulate other people in positive ways. This can help us gain an advantage in our lives, businesses, and law enforcement.

Although we believe that everyone in the world is honest and good-hearted, humans all have their weaknesses and "dark sides." Everyone has a blindside. It's up for us to learn about it and protect it. Dark Psychology is prevalent in the world, and it's impossible to trust anyone, even if you are dishonest.

If you are honest with someone, they will tell the truth without being asked for any advice.

I hope this book will help me recognize situations in the future and to protect myself from being manipulated by or attacked.

People who are able and able to see manipulation and recognize it is important. It's often too late for us to realize that we have been mistreated. There are many techniques that can be used to manipulate, control, or read another person. Although I'm certain that some of my techniques could be used for beneficial purposes, it's best to not use them on other people.

It's far better to find out how this dark psychology works and what you could do to avoid being manipulated. The information in this book can be dangerous and I hope you use it wisely.

Dark Psychology has always been a problem. This book teaches you how to avoid manipulation so you can live a happy life.

I thank you for reading this book. I hope that you learn something new.

www.ingramcontent.com/pod-product-compliance
Lightning Source LLC
Chambersburg PA
CBHW050408120526
44590CB00015B/1879